Disney Cruise Line

Wendy Lefkon
EDITORIAL DIRECTOR

Jill Safro
EDITOR

Debbie Lofaso
DESIGNER

Lois Spritzer
WRITER

Jessica Ward
ASSISTANT EDITOR

Jody Revenson
CONSULTING EDITOR

Alexandra Mayes Birnbaum
CONSULTING EDITOR

THE OFFICIAL GUIDE

DISNEP EDITIONS

NEW YORK

AN IMPRINT OF DISNEY BOOK GROUP

For Steve Birnbaum, who merely made all this possible.

Copyright © 2008 Disney Enterprises, Inc.

All photographs and artwork copyright © 2008 Disney Enterprises, Inc.

Additional text by Jill Safro

Maps by Gregory Wakabayashi

Cover photograph by Mike Carroll

ISBN: 978-1-4231-1051-4

Printed in the United States of America

Other 2009 Birnbaum's Official Disney Guides

Disneyland

Walt Disney World

Walt Disney World Dining

Walt Disney World For Kids

Walt Disney World Pocket Parks Guide

Walt Disney World Without Kids

A WORD FROM THE EDITOR

Birnbaum editors are notoriously proud of their knowledge when it comes to all things Disney. After all, we've been gathering expertise about Disney theme parks for more decades than we care to admit. But luxury ocean liners? Tropical islands? Foreign ports of call? These represented some seriously uncharted waters for us . . . until we created this, our annually updated official guide to Disney Cruise Line. After comprehensive, grueling (yeah, right) research, we happily boast expert status in this area, and we're eager to share what we've learned.

For starters, we quickly realized that a voyage with the Mouse is atypical in a number of ways. Most obviously, there's the simultaneous (and successful) catering to families with kids and grown-ups *sans* offspring. In fact, each ship has programming designed to draw young, old, and those in between to entirely different recreational areas. Then there's the innovative "rotational dining system," a lineup of lavish musical productions, deck-shaking dance parties with Disney characters, and, of course, the unique grand finale: a full day at Castaway Cay—a private, almost-too-good-to-be-true tropical island.

Like swaying in a hammock in the aforementioned paradise, the idea of purchasing a vacation package may lull one into an "everything is taken care of" sense of security. The truth is, there are still dozens of decisions to make, staterooms to select, shore excursions to book, etc. Within these pages, as with any Birnbaum guide, you'll find detailed, accurate information meant to help you plan a successful vacation.

Of course, even with our rigorous research missions (which, incidentally, began with the inaugural sailing of the *Disney Magic* in the summer of 1998), this book would not exist without the contributions of so many. To begin with, we owe a big thank-you to the folks at Disney Cruise Line. Although all editorial decisions are made by the editor, it's their willingness to explain operations and provide factual data that makes this the Official Guide.

In particular, I'd like to extend a boatload of gratitude to Meredith Renard, Marcy Storm, Jara Church, Heath William Stewart, Paul Sost, Pierre-Marie Leprince, Lisa Broschart, Erin Jackson, Maureen Landry, David Baldree, Kathryn Hart, Larry Stauffer, and Alison Mahoney—and especially to Jason Lasecki for the care and effort that he has put into this project.

For their key roles behind the scenes, we salute Nisha Panchal, Jill Rapaport, Warren Meislin, Gabrielle Bill, Michelle Olveira, Amy Henning, and Mike Carroll.

Of course, no list of acknowledgments is complete without our founding editor, Steve Birnbaum, as well as Alexandra Mayes Birnbaum, who continues to provide gentle guidance and invaluable insight.

Finally, it's important to remember that specifics do change. To that end, we refine and expand our material with each annual revision. For the present edition, though, this is the final word.

Bon Voyage!

WHAT DO YOU THINK?

Nothing is more valuable to us than your comments on what we've written and on your own experiences with Disney Cruise Line. Please share your insights with us by writing to:

Birnbaum's Official Guide to Disney Cruise Line, 2009
Disney Editions
114 Fifth Avenue, 14th Floor
New York, NY 10011
Attn: Jill Safro

TABLE OF CONTENTS

BEFORE YOU SAIL   6

Read this and you'll have everything you need to know before you go—Disney Cruise Line itineraries, how to select a cruise package, stateroom specifics, packing pointers, and much more.

ALL ABOARD   42

This deck-by-deck view of the *Disney Magic* and the *Disney Wonder* takes you on a stem-to-stern tour, starting with check-in and finishing with a visit to the spa. By the time you board, the ship should feel like home.

PORTS OF CALL   100

Here's a brief background about each port visited by Disney Cruise Line, peppered with information about every shore excursion available, plus our first-hand accounts, to help you choose which shore tours to take and which you can skip.

LAND AND SEA VACATIONS   202

Can't decide between a stay at Walt Disney World or a voyage aboard Disney Cruise Line? Why not combine the two? This chapter explains how to get the most out of a "land and sea" vacation package and how to customize your trip.

BEFORE YOU SAIL

Planning Ahead

The fact that you are holding this book means that you have probably decided to make Disney your cruise vacation choice. Now comes the hard part: Which cruise package is best for you? How do you book it? What should you do to prepare for the voyage? The information that follows should answer these questions and help—whether this is your first cruise or your fiftieth—take the idea of a Disney Cruise from concept to reality.

Selecting a Cruise

What to do, what to do. There are many factors to consider when choosing a cruise package. Among the most important are budget, time available, stateroom needs, and preferred itinerary.

If you want to take the most inexpensive cruise possible, then a 3-night cruise in a standard inside stateroom is probably a good choice. If money is no object, consider a 7-night adventure in the super-deluxe Walt Disney Suite. Of course, there are plenty of things in between—including pairing a Disney Cruise with a stay at Walt Disney World (see page 203). As for itineraries, choose from 3-, 4-, and 7-night options. What follows is a rundown of the various itineraries as they were available at press time.

ITINERARIES*

3-Night Bahamian Cruise	
DAY	ITINERARY
Thursday	Check in at Port Canaveral Terminal. Aboard by 4 P.M.
Friday	Ashore at Nassau at 9:30 A.M. Aboard by 7 P.M.
Saturday	Ashore at Castaway Cay at 8:30 A.M. Aboard by 5 P.M.
Sunday	Ship at Port Canaveral beginning at 7:30 A.M.

4-Night Bahamian Cruise	
DAY	ITINERARY
Sunday	Check in at Port Canaveral Terminal. Aboard by 4 P.M.
Monday	Ashore at Nassau at 9:30 A.M. Aboard by 7 P.M.
Tuesday	Ashore at Castaway Cay at 8:30 A.M. Aboard by 5 P.M.
Wednesday	Full day at sea.
Thursday	Ship at Port Canaveral beginning at 7:30 A.M.

*All itineraries and times were correct at press time, but are subject to change.

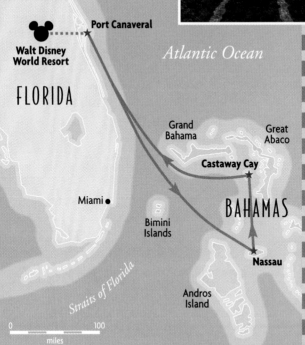

Port Canaveral

Walt Disney
World Resort

Atlantic Ocean

FLORIDA

Grand
Bahama

Great
Abaco

Castaway Cay

Miami

BAHAMAS

Bimini
Islands

Nassau

Straits of Florida

Andros
Island

0   100
miles

7-Night Western Caribbean Cruise

DAY	ITINERARY
Saturday	Check in at Port Canaveral Terminal. Aboard by 4 P.M.
Sunday	Ashore at Key West at 11:30 A.M. Aboard by 7:30 P.M.
Monday	Full day at sea.
Tuesday	Ashore at Grand Cayman at 7:30 A.M. Aboard by 4:30 P.M.
Wednesday	Ashore in Cozumel at 9:30 A.M. Aboard by 6:30 P.M.
Thursday	Full day at sea.
Friday	Ashore at Castaway Cay at 9:30 A.M. Aboard by 5 P.M.
Saturday	Ship at Port Canaveral beginning at 7:35 A.M.

7-Night Eastern Caribbean Cruise: Itinerary A

DAY	ITINERARY
Saturday	Check in at Port Canaveral Terminal. Aboard by 4 P.M.
Sunday	Full day at sea.
Monday	Full day at sea.
Tuesday	Ashore in St. Maarten at 8 A.M. Aboard by 7 P.M.
Wednesday	Ashore in St. Thomas at 8 A.M. (It's possible to experience excursions to St. John, too.) Aboard by 4:30 P.M.
Thursday	Full day at sea.
Friday	Ashore at Castaway Cay at 9:30 A.M. Aboard by 5 P.M.
Saturday	Ship at Port Canaveral beginning at 7:35 A.M.

7-Night Eastern Caribbean Cruise: Itinerary B

DAY	ITINERARY
Saturday	Check in at Port Canaveral Terminal. Aboard by 4 P.M.
Sunday	Full day at sea.
Monday	Full day at sea.
Tuesday	Ashore in St. Croix at 7:30 A.M. Aboard by 4 P.M.
Wednesday	Ashore in St. Thomas at 7:30 A.M. (It's possible to visit St. John, too.) Aboard by 4:30 P.M.
Thursday	Full day at sea.
Friday	Ashore at Castaway Cay at 9:30 A.M. Aboard by 5 P.M.
Saturday	Ship at Port Canaveral beginning at 7:35 A.M.

7-Night Eastern Caribbean Cruise: Itinerary C

DAY	ITINERARY
Saturday	Check in at Port Canaveral Terminal. Aboard by 4 P.M.
Sunday	Full day at sea.
Monday	Full day at sea.
Tuesday	Ashore in Tortola at 7:30 A.M. Aboard by 7 P.M.
Wednesday	Ashore in St. Thomas at 8 A.M. (It's possible to experience excursions to St. John, too.) Aboard by 4:30 P.M.
Thursday	Full day at sea.
Friday	Ashore at Castaway Cay at 9:30 A.M. Aboard by 5 P.M.
Saturday	Ship at Port Canaveral beginning at 7:35 A.M.

7-Night Land and Sea Vacation (with 3-night cruise)

DAY	ITINERARY
Sunday–Wednesday	Enjoy a stay at a Walt Disney World resort.
Thursday	Check in at Port Canaveral Terminal. Aboard ship by 4 P.M.
Friday	Ashore at Nassau at 9:30 A.M. Aboard by 7 P.M.
Saturday	Ashore at Castaway Cay at 8:30 A.M. Aboard by 5 P.M.
Sunday	Ship at Port Canaveral beginning at 7:35 A.M.

7-Night Land and Sea Vacation (with 4-night cruise)

DAY	ITINERARY
Thursday–Saturday	Enjoy a stay at a Walt Disney World resort.
Sunday	Travel to Port Canaveral Terminal. Aboard by 4 P.M.
Monday	Ashore at Nassau at 9:30 A.M. Aboard by 7 P.M.
Tuesday	Ashore at Castaway Cay at 8:30 A.M. Aboard by 5 P.M.
Wednesday	Full day at sea.
Thursday	Ship at Port Canaveral beginning at 7:35 A.M.

Check Your Calendar

Determining the length of your cruise depends on several things—the first, and most obvious, being how much time you have in your busy schedule to devote to leisure. If your answer is only three or four days, don't despair: The *Disney Wonder* sails to the Bahamas with stops at Nassau and Disney's own private, tropical island, Castaway Cay. If you have a week, you also have choices: the *Disney Magic* offers seven-night cruises to the Eastern and Western Caribbean. So, if you've done St. Maarten and St. Thomas to death, consider St. Croix or Tortola. Or head west to Cozumel and Grand Cayman. And, if you're lucky enough to have a lot of time available, you could take back-to-back weeklong sails to both the Eastern and Western Caribbean

(the *Magic* alternates between them). There may be special destination cruises from time to time, but these (if any) were not determined at press time. For updates, call 800-910-3659 or visit Disney Cruise Line's Web site: *www.disneycruise.com*.

Check Your Checkbook

The cost of your cruise is the next issue on the planning board. Budgetary constraints can be eased in several ways: by taking one of the shorter cruises, choosing a less expensive cabin class, and by limiting the number of land tours and excursions you take at the various ports of call. Plan to eat aboard the ship, too—meals and snacks are included in every vacation package, as are many extras, including stage shows, movies, tours, lectures, games, bands, deck parties with characters, and more.

DISNEY CRUISE LINE RATES

LENGTH OF CRUISE	ITINERARY	RATE RANGE
⚓ 3 nights	Nassau/Castaway Cay	$429–$2,999 (adult) $229–$1,099 (child age 3–12) $149 (under age 3*)
⚓ 4 nights	Nassau/Castaway Cay	$499–$3,999 (adult) $329–$1,199 (child age 3–12) $149 (under age 3*)
⚓ 7 nights	Western: Key West, Grand Cayman, Cozumel, Castaway Cay Eastern: St. Maarten, St. Thomas/St. John, Castaway Cay; St. Croix, St. Thomas/St. John, Castaway Cay; Tortola, St. Thomas/St. John, Castaway Cay	$849–$5,399 (adult) $399–$2,199 (child age 3–12) $189 (under age 3*)
⚓ 7–night Land and Sea	Walt Disney World and Sea Vacation (with 3 days at WDW and 4-night cruise or 4 days at WDW and 3-night cruise)	$939–$5,399 (adult) $399–$2,199 (child 3–12) $189 (under age 3*)

*Babies younger than 12 weeks are not permitted to travel.
Prices do not include tax and were correct at press time, but are subject to change. Expect them to increase during the year.

DID YOU KNOW?

The 1,367 miles of cable onboard would be enough to run an extension cord between Texas and Michigan.

WHAT'S NOT INCLUDED

Rest assured that all of your basic vacation needs are covered by the "all-inclusive" price of the cruise. However, there are always "extras" that you may want to ante up a little cash for. Here's a list of items and services that carry an extra charge:

- Babysitting (See pages 30 and 89)
- Shore excursions
- Expenses incurred while on land in ports of call (with the exception of food and soft drinks at Castaway Cay)
- Tipping on the ship (Refer to "Tipping" on page 41)
- Alcoholic beverages
- Palo (Dining at this optional, exceptional, reservations-necessary, adults-only restaurant costs $15 per person for dinner and brunch and $5 per person for high tea.)
- Refreshments at Cove Cafe, The Stack, Aloft, and at any bar
- Spa treatments
- Arcade games
- Photographs snapped by the ship's photographers
- Internet usage (See page 38)
- Cell phone usage (See page 38)
- Ship-to-shore telephone calls (There is a sizable fee for all calls, incoming and outgoing. Calls within the ship are free.)

With the exception of non-Disney ports of call, all "incidental" charges will be billed to your stateroom, provided that you leave a credit card imprint upon check-in. It's a good idea to have some cash on hand (we bring about $300, just in case), but there are few chances to use it. Except for tips, it isn't accepted on the ships. Same goes for Castaway Cay, with the exception of the post office—stamps must be purchased with cash. Most of the non-Disney port shops accept major credit cards, and most accept U.S. currency.

Selecting a Stateroom

Sure, you'd like the largest suite on the ship. No question, you want the biggest veranda. And, of course, you absolutely must have a great view. But if that doesn't fit within your budget, there are other appealing options. Consider this: Every stateroom boasts nautical decor, has ample closet space, a television, and a small safe. Inside state-rooms are much less expensive and not a whole lot smaller than their outside counterparts. On the other hand, should you decide to splurge, know that there are larger suites with private verandas where you can sip a refreshing beverage or read the newest page-turner, periodically taking a moment to gaze at the sea.

Of course, there are other factors to think about when selecting a stateroom. How many people are in your party? Are you traveling with young children? Perhaps a spacious suite would suit your family's needs. These accommodations have queen-size beds, bunk beds for the kids, and a split bath (see page 57). A curtained divider provides a bit of privacy.

WHAT'S IN A NAME?

A whole lot, when it comes to the names of Disney Cruise Line accommodations. Here's a listing of the types of rooms, with the most cost-efficient first. Note that it is possible to request side-by-side staterooms, but it can't be guaranteed. For specifics on stateroom amenities, refer to page 56.

⚓ Standard Inside Stateroom

⚓ Deluxe Inside Stateroom

⚓ Deluxe Ocean-view Stateroom

⚓ Deluxe Stateroom with Navigator's Veranda (enclosed veranda)

⚓ Deluxe Stateroom with Veranda (open veranda)

⚓ Deluxe Family Stateroom with Veranda

⚓ 1-Bedroom Suite with Veranda

⚓ 2-Bedroom Suite with Veranda

⚓ Royal Suite with Veranda

(For more details about staterooms, turn to the *All Aboard* chapter, which begins on page 42.) Of course, there's always the Walt Disney Suite and the Roy E. Disney Suite—so if money is absolutely no object, treat your crew to one of these thousand-square-foot homes away from home. No matter what your accommodations requirements are, chances are Disney Cruise Line can meet them.

DID YOU KNOW?

The Disney ships can make 500,000 gallons of fresh water from seawater every day while cruising.

How to Book a Cruise

In addition to using *www.disneycruise.com* or contacting Disney Cruise Line (800-910-3659), many guests book through travel agents.

PAYMENT METHODS

Cruise packages, as well as incidentals, gratuities, hotel bills, and deposits may be paid by credit card (Visa, MasterCard, JCB Card, American Express, Diners Club, Disney Visa, etc.), traveler's check, cashier's check, money order, cash, or personal check. Checks must bear the guest's name and address, be drawn on a U.S. bank, and be accompanied by proper ID (a valid driver's license with photo or government-issued photo ID). Keep in mind that final payment for the cruise package must be made *at least 90 days* before your vacation commencement date. Personal checks should be mailed to the following address:

ALL GOOD THINGS . . .

How time flies when you're having fun. No sooner can you find your way around the ship without even looking at a map—it's time to go home. Here are a few things you should know about the debarkation process.

A day or so before your arrival back at Port Canaveral, you'll receive an information packet that includes a set of colored luggage tags. The color coding designates the area of the terminal at which you can pick them up. Be sure to remove the original tags from the inbound trip before you put new tags on all bags. (Guest Services has extra tags.) You will also receive a U.S. Customs form to fill out. You will hand this form in as you leave.

On the night before debarkation, you'll have to put all your checked luggage outside your stateroom before 11 P.M. (Bags will be collected and delivered to a color-coded area at the terminal.) Keep valuables, medications, tickets, passports, and other important documents with you to put in your carry-on bags. At dinner on your last night, your waitstaff will tell you where and when breakfast will be served the next morning. Once breakfast is done, it's time to grab your belongings and head off the ship, taking all your happy memories and, quite possibly, the promise to return again soon.

Disney Cruise Vacations
P. O. Box 277763
Atlanta, GA 30384-7763;
cashier's checks should be
sent to:
Disney Cruise Vacations
Attn.: Cash Operations
P. O. Box 10155
Lake Buena Vista, FL 32830

DEPOSIT REQUIREMENTS

When you book a trip, you'll
get a "due date" for a deposit.
The deposit is $200–$400
per person for a 3- or 4-night
cruise, and $250–$500 for a

WWW.DISNEYCRUISE.COM

We've done our best to provide
accurate, current information
regarding all things Disney Cruise
Line. That said, rates, itineraries,
excursions, and other specifics are
subject to change. For more
information or to book a cruise or
excursion, visit the new and
improved, interactive Web site:
www.disneycruise.com. The site is
one of the most comprehensive
and user-friendly Web sites we
have ever seen.

7-night cruise. Reservations
will be canceled if a deposit
is not received by the
deadline. (Packages booked
less than 75 days before
arrival get special instructions.)

CANCELLATION POLICY

Though cancellations may
be made by telephone or by
mail, we suggest the phone.

For categories 1–3,
deposits are non-refundable.
If you cancel a cruise
between 8 and 44 days
before commencement date,
you will be charged half the
cost of the package. Should
you cancel within 7 days of
commencement, you will be
refunded tax only.

For categories 4–12,
deposits are fully refundable
if the trip is canceled more
than 75 days ahead. Cancel
after 75 days and you'll have
to eat the deposit. Cancellations made between 8
and 44 days prior to the
commencement date (all
categories) will set you back

half the cost of the cruise package (per guest). Cancel within 7 days of commencement and there will be no refund of cruise fare (just tax). To avoid this fate, insure your trip (see page 24).

What to Pack

"Cruise Casual" is almost always the operative phrase with Disney. Shorts, T-shirts, sundresses, and the like are fine daytime wear. At dinnertime, casual takes on a more formal meaning: Set aside the shorts and plan on slacks (jeans are okay, except at Palo) and a collared shirt for men, with real shoes, as opposed to those of the tennis variety. The same goes for women, while dresses are suitable, too. On 7-night cruises, there is a semi-formal and a formal night. While some folks don black tie and sequins, it's not necessary to break out formal wear if you prefer a more casual look. On

HOT TIP

Guests who plan to arrive at Port Canaveral the night before setting sail might consider staying at one of these resorts on nearby Astronaut Boulevard:

• Country Inns & Suites by Carlson: Rates range from $89–$149, and there is a shuttle to the cruise terminal; 321-784-8500 or 888-201-1746.

• Residence Inn by Marriott: Rates range from $169–$199; 321-323-1100 or 800-331-3131.

these occasions, the *Personal Navigator* will tip you off as to the appropriate attire. Many guests pack pirate garb, too, in anticipation of Pirates IN the Caribbean party night.

Bathing suits are a must, as are beach shoes, wraps, sunscreen, sunglasses, and hats. Some sundries, including shampoo, conditioner, and lotion, are provided in your stateroom.

Others are available for purchase, but the prices are steep, and the shops aren't always open (U.S. Customs limits their operating hours). Take an inventory of the products you'll need daily, and be sure to take them. Here's a checklist of additional must-haves: proper documentation (a passport is ideal), cash, film or memory cards, waterproof ID holder, prescription medication (in original containers), at least one "dressy" outfit, and comfortable shoes.

Pack a Day Bag

Guests may check in and board the *Disney Wonder* or *Disney Magic* as early as 1 P.M., but your luggage may not arrive until 6 P.M. (though usually earlier). Keep in mind that you will have access to your stateroom throughout the day, along with most shipboard amenities, including all pools. Rather than travel in your

swimsuit, pack it in a special day bag. This should serve as, or fit in, a carry-on, as all checked bags will be out of your hands once you surrender them. (It can't be larger than 9 inches by 14 inches by 22 inches, and does not count as part of the two-bag-per-passenger quota.) The bag should include ID, valuables, shorts, swimsuits, grooming supplies, hats, sunscreen, and anything else you'll need during those first hours onboard. Put breakable items in your day bag, too.

HOT TIP

Each guest may bring two pieces of luggage, plus a carry-on bag and a purse or briefcase aboard. The more compact the bags, the better—it'll free up more room for *you* inside your stateroom!

Booking Shore Excursions

All prospective Disney Cruise Line guests receive an advance list of the tours and activities that are offered at each port of call, so it makes sense to sign up before you sail. Our *Ports of Call* chapter offers a description of each excursion, along with a personal reaction. Tours fill up early, so reserve your favorites as soon as possible. Cancellations or changes may be made up to 3 days before the start of the cruise to receive a full refund. After that, you pay whether you play or not.

To book your shore excursions (aka "port adventures") in advance, visit *www.disneycruise.com*. Excursions may be canceled up to three days prior to vacation commencement to get a full refund. To make last-minute arrangements, visit your ship's Port Adventures desk.

IDENTIFICATION PAPERS

Unlike a visit to Walt Disney World's Epcot, where it only feels as if you're leaving the country, in the case of a Disney Cruise Line vacation, you really do. Given that, you'll need to provide proper proof of citizenship when passing through customs. Since U.S. government passport requirements keep changing, we strongly encourage all guests to have a valid passport for all cruises. It's just easier that way. Visit *http://travel.state.gov* or call 877-487-2778 for the most current requirements.

HOT TIP

You will always have to show your "Key to the World" card (Disney-issued stateroom key and ID) when disembarking or boarding the ship. Adults also need a government-issued photo ID (a passport is ideal).

INSURE YOUR TRIP

Nobody books a vacation expecting to cancel it—yet sometimes life intervenes and it's unavoidable. That's why we strongly recommend that you make travel insurance a part of your vacation budget. (We do.) The Disney Cruise Line Vacation Plan provides baggage, trip cancellation/interruption, and medical-expense coverage for the duration of your cruise. The cost of the plan is calculated per guest. At press time, rates were $59 for the first and second guest, $39 per additional guest for a 3-night cruise; $69 for the first two guests, $49 per extra guest for a 4-night cruise; and $109 for the first two guests, $59 per additional guest for a 7-night cruise or land and sea package. Here's an overview of what's covered:

⚓ Trip cancellation/interruption protection (for medical reasons or other specific issues)

⚓ Travel-delay protection (for additional travel expenses incurred by you due to covered travel delays)

⚓ Emergency medical/dental benefits for the duration of your cruise (includes transportation to the nearest appropriate medical facility)

⚓ Baggage coverage (for lost or delayed arrival of baggage)

⚓ A 24-hour hotline to help with replacement of lost travel documents or emergency cash transfers. (From the U.S.,call 800-573-5665; outside the U.S., call 804-673-1159. Mention Disney Cruise Line group number 2043; ID 00100287.)

How to Get There

By Plane

Fly to Orlando International Airport. We like to book a flight that is scheduled to arrive in the mid-morning. Why? Because that lets you check in at Port Canaveral and board the ship as early as 1 P.M. If you get there on the early side, you can make a day of it. And, if your flight is delayed, you'll still have a shot at making it to Port Canaveral before the ship sails. (3:30 P.M. is the cutoff time for checking in. Don't be late!)

At the Airport

As you get off the shuttle and enter the main terminal (after a tram ride), proceed directly to the Disney Welcome Center. It's located on Level 1, Side B of the terminal. Expect a Disney representative to collect all paperwork and escort you to a motor coach. Don't worry about luggage. All bags bearing the appropriate tags will be claimed and loaded onto the bus for you. (If you are driving to the ship, refer to page 26.)

COLD AND FLU ADVISORY

Disney Cruise Line follows extraordinary sanitation efforts to ensure the safety and comfort of guests. Even so, people can get sick. If you or a member of your party experience any symptom of illness (cold, flu, etc.) within 72 hours of sailing, it's best if you postpone your trip. (Disney Cruise Line reps will direct you to someone who will help arrange an alternative Walt Disney World vacation.)

Once onboard, all guests are asked to wash their hands frequently and thoroughly—as this is a highly effective barrier to spreading germs. If you or someone in your party does become ill during your trip, head directly to the Medical Center. You'll be taken care of there, and immediate treatment will help limit the potential impact to others.

and follow signs to Cruise Terminal 8.

Drivers originating in South Florida should take I-95 North. Exit at #205 for S.R. 528 East (The Beachline). Take S.R. 528 to S.R. 401. Stay right and follow signs to Terminal 8.

Getting to Port Canaveral from WDW (without a Car)

Disney Cruise Line has dedicated buses to chauffeur guests directly from selected Walt Disney World resorts. They are: the Grand Floridian, Animal Kingdom Lodge, Polynesian, Beach Club, Port Orleans Riverside, Port Orleans French Quarter,

IMPORTANT NUMBERS
• Disney Cruise Line reservations and information: 800-910-3659
• Walt Disney World Central Reservations: 407-934-7639

Caribbean Beach, Saratoga Springs, BoardWalk, Wilderness Lodge, Old Key West, and Swan and Dolphin resorts. Be sure to allow plenty of time for travel. One-way transfers cost $35 per person, while $69 will cover the round trip. On the morning of departure, guests should contact bell services for luggage pick-up and verify motor coach departure time. (Car services make the trip, too. See page 26 for contact information.)

Customized Travel Tips

Traveling with Babies
CRIBS

If you are traveling with a baby, it is possible to have a playpen-like, foldaway crib sent to your state-room. (The cribs are 39.8 inches long, 28.25 inches wide, and 31.25 inches high.) Request one when you make a reservation, and

confirm it before leaving home. (If you booked your cruise package through a travel agent, call said agent with special requests such as this.) Supplies are limited. Bring your own baby bedding, as the cribs come with fitted sheets only.

FOOD

All staterooms have a "cooling box," which maintains a temperature of approximately 55 degrees. Formula and food can be stored safely within the unit. At least one shop onboard sells diapers and a small selection of formula. If you'd like to save money, pack as many baby rations as

possible. Round-the-clock room service means you will never get caught with a screaming, hungry little one and no means of quelling the hunger pangs.

BABYSITTING

Onboard babysitting is available for tots ages 12 weeks to 3 years. The cost is $6 an hour for the first child, with a two-hour minimum. Each additional child (who must be a sibling) is $5 per hour. The service is offered at Flounder's Reef Nursery. Reservations may be made at *www.disneycruise.com* or on-board (based on availability). In-room babysitting is not offered on either ship.

OTHER SUPPLIES

Diapers, pacifiers, pool toys, and more can be purchased onboard. The shops aren't always open, so take inventory to avoid being caught short. If it's an emergency, inquire at

Guest Services. They can help with just about any onboard crisis.

Travelers with Disabilities

Measures have been taken to make your stay as comfortable and effortless as possible. Each ship has 16 staterooms that are equipped for guests using wheelchairs. They have ramped bathroom thresholds, open bed frames, bathroom and shower handrails, fold-down shower seats, hand-held showerheads, and lowered towel and closet bars. Closed-captioning is available for stateroom TVs and some onboard video monitors. Stateroom Communication Kits may be reserved upon request. They include door-knock and phone alerts, phone amplifier, bed shaker notification, a strobe light smoke detector, and a text typewriter (TTY). There is

MEDICINE STORAGE

All staterooms come equipped with "cooling boxes." They are perfectly suited to storing food, but not medication (especially if the medicine requires a stable temperature). Guests who need to store medicine should visit the onboard medical center or request a compact refrigerator. The number is quite limited, so be sure to ask for one at the same time you reserve your cruise package. Call to confirm it before you leave.

HOT TIP

There is a small number of wheelchairs to borrow for use onboard, but if you'll be using a wheelchair for the entire trip (including ports of call), you should bring your own.

GETTING AROUND IT

Disabled travelers already know that travel requires a lot of advance planning. Disney has equipped its ships with a variety of amenities geared toward those guests with special needs.

Wheelchair-accessible staterooms are equipped with ramp entrances to bathrooms, fold-down shower seats, handheld shower heads, lowered towel and closet racks, a bathroom phone, and Emergency Call buttons.

There is a limited number of sand wheelchairs available (first come, first served). Note: If you will need a wheelchair throughout the cruise, you are encouraged to bring your own.

Throughout the ship, there are signs indicating the location of wheelchair-accessible restrooms.

Hearing-impaired guests need not miss any of the fun onboard. In-cabin TVs can be equipped with closed-captioning and assisted-listening devices are available at all theaters and show rooms. Also available are communication kits equipped with strobe light smoke alarms, door-knock and telephone alerts, and TTY (a text typewriter). Make your needs known when you book your cruise.

no extra charge for the kit, but supplies are limited. Request it when you make your reservation and confirm it prior to sailing.

Wheelchair-accessible restrooms are available in several common areas onboard the ship. There are transfer tiers at the Quiet Cove pool. (Each is a multistep tier and is not automatic. To use it, a guest must be able to lift themselves out of his or her chair.) Sand wheelchairs are available at Castaway Cay. American Sign Language interpretation is available for live performances on select cruise dates. (The service is not available on every cruise, so be sure to start planning your trip well in advance.) For additional information or to make special requests, ask your reservationist. For more information via TTY, call 407-566-7455.

Travelers without Children

This being a Disney cruise, one could argue that you—the footloose, fancy-free folks—are on their turf. And, as such, you might expect to have youngsters underfoot at all times. This is simply not the case. The Disney ships were designed with three specific types of vacationers in mind: families, kids, and grown-ups without kids. Onboard, there is an adults-only deck area, complete with its own pool (not to mention music and games).

There's a romantic, gourmet restaurant and a cozy coffee bar. It goes without saying that those spots, as well as several lounges, are strictly for the grown-up set (as in adults with legal proof of age). Plus, there are countless other ways to enjoy a grown-up

getaway in the various ports of call. With that in mind, Castaway Cay (Disney's private island) guarantees you and your ilk a piece of beachfront real estate where you can bask in the sun or read a novel in the shade without the fear of sand being kicked in your face. You can even have a massage in a private cabana overlooking the ocean.

Can you manage to spend days on end without encountering the wee ones of our species? No way. But who'd want to?

Medical Matters

The Medical Center, located forward on Deck 1, is open daily to assist with any medical emergencies or health concerns. Regular hours are from 9:30 A.M. to 11 A.M. and from 4:30 P.M. to 7 P.M. Both the *Magic* and the *Wonder* have a physician and nurse on call 24 hours a day (even while in port) for conditions requiring immediate attention. Health services are provided by a company independent from Disney Cruise Line, and standard prevailing fees will be charged for all services. Fees will be charged to your stateroom account.

In extreme cases, Disney Cruise Line will arrange to have a passenger taken to the nearest port to receive medical care. The cost of this varies with the location of the ship and the nearest port. Because all care provided qualifies as "care outside the United States," you will be responsible for paying any charges incurred while onboard prior to debarkation and submitting the request for coverage to your insurance carrier (paperwork will be provided).

If you get sick while on shore, your guide should direct you back to your ship's tour director at the dock—who will help you get back to the ship.

If you are a diabetic using insulin or take other medication that needs to be refrigerated during your cruise, you can arrange for a small refrigerator to be brought to your cabin. Make your needs known well in advance. Take a supply of all prescription medicines with you, as the ship does not have a pharmacy. (Always travel with medicines in their original containers.)

Regarding younger passengers, know that a child exhibiting symptoms of illness will not be allowed to participate in youth activities or be cared for in Flounder's Reef Nursery.

IT'S NOT EASY BEING GREEN

Unfortunately, Mother Nature being predictably unpredictable, the seas are occasionally a tad turbulent. So, there's always the possibility that you or a member of your party may become a little green about the gills. Plan ahead. We recommend packing a supply of over-the-counter medication (but know these may make you drowsy). We also suggest you pack ginger pills (available at most health food and vitamin stores) and drink ginger ale.

If you've experienced motion sickness in the past, try to steer clear of inside cabins. Outer cabins have windows—and the view of the horizon can be a helpful stabilizer. If the room has a veranda, all the better. Fresh air may not be an antidote to nausea, but it can't hurt. Some have found relief in the form of bitters mixed with water or club soda. Then there are sea bands. They fit snugly around the wrist, supposedly alleviating symptoms by hitting key acupressure points. You can pick them up at many pharmacies.

If all else fails, be aware that sea-sickness bags are available. The good news is, most people get their "sea legs" very quickly, adjusting to the motion (slight or otherwise) soon after setting sail.

35

Special Occasions

For many travelers, taking a cruise is a special occasion in and of itself. Still, lots of folks choose to celebrate birthdays, anniversaries, and other special events onboard. If you fall into this category, be sure to tell your travel agent or alert Disney Cruise Line three weeks before you sail. That will ensure that your dining room staff will acknowledge your happy occasion over dinner. Some occasions, such as weddings and family reunions, require a bit more preplanning.

Weddings

Whether you are saying your "I do's" for the first time, committing yourselves to one another, or renewing your vows, Disney Cruise Line has the means to make the occasion exceptionally memorable. Ceremonies may be performed on the ship or at Castaway Cay.

Some happy couples invite family members along for the trip, while others prefer to have this time to themselves. For more information, contact your travel agent or a Disney wedding consultant at 407-828-3400. Call as far in advance as possible.

Honeymoons

Just married? If so, you may want to make more of this memorable moment by purchasing Disney's Romantic Escape. For an additional $359 or so per couple (on 3-, 4-, and 7-night cruises), you will receive a special romantic

basket delivered to your room, one night's "romance turndown service," a champagne breakfast in bed, a Tropical Rainforest pass to Vista Spa & Salon, and a romantic dinner for two at Palo. Note that you need not be newlyweds to enjoy the "Romantic Escape."

Reunions

Whether you are reuniting 8 or 80 members of the family, Disney Cruise Line can host your entire party. Simply request the Family Reunion Option when you book your cruise. Each member of the party will receive a personalized Disney Cruise Line reunion T-shirt, each cabin gets a leather photo album with one complimentary photo and a commemorative Disney reunion certificate. At press time, the reunion perks cost an extra $59 for the first two family members and $19 per

person for each additional guest for a 3-, or 4-night cruise. For information, contact a travel agent or call 800-910-3659.

The aforementioned packages are fully refundable if canceled up to 30 days before the cruise. After that, there are no refunds issued.

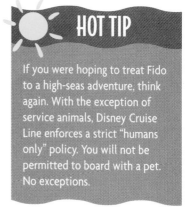

HOT TIP

If you were hoping to treat Fido to a high-seas adventure, think again. With the exception of service animals, Disney Cruise Line enforces a strict "humans only" policy. You will not be permitted to board with a pet. No exceptions.

Disney Cruise Line guests may be contacted by calling 888-322-8732 from the U.S. The international number is 1-732-335-3281. Ship-to-shore telephone rates apply. Those rates range from about $7 to $9.50 per minute. Callers should have the ship name and the name of the party they are contacting. To specify the ship, they would select 1 for the *Disney Magic*, and 2 for the *Disney Wonder*. Payment may be made by credit card. Messages can be recorded via voice mail.

Some guests may also be reached by personal cell phone. Wireless service, available in staterooms only, is available to subscribers of a host of cellular providers worldwide. Rates vary.

HOT TIP

If you plan to use your cell phone during your cruise, be sure to check with your wireless provider before leaving home. Ask if you'll get service through them while onboard and how much said service costs.

Fingertip Reference Guide

Business Services

Wait a minute, aren't you here to relax? For those of you who must get a little work done while at sea, there are some business services available for an additional charge. Among them are fax transmission, copies, and AV equipment. There is Internet access (for a fee) at the Internet Cafe (adjacent to Promenade Lounge) and the Cove Cafe (where there are four "loaner" laptops); staterooms have phones (ship-to-shore rates apply); and electrical outlets are laptop friendly. Note that the ships' computers are not equipped to accept uploads. There is, however, a handy printer at the ready. Stateroom wireless Internet service is available (for a fee) to guests with wireless-ready laptops.

Camera Needs

By all means, bring a camera. Film and memory cards are sold onboard and at many ports of call. Keep in mind that all undeveloped film should be packed in carry-on bags, or risk having it destroyed by airport scanners.

There are also many photographers wandering about the ship, capturing moments throughout the day. You'll find the photos displayed for purchase at Shutters, the onboard photo store. This is also the place to transfer digital photos to a CD (for a fee).

Drinking Laws

The drinking age on the ship is 21 and is strictly enforced. Valid photo ID is required. Disney Cruise Line reserves the right to refuse alcohol sales to anyone.

Mail

Letters and postcards may be mailed from the post office at Castaway Cay. Stamps are the only things available for purchase here (cash only). It's also possible to mail items from other ports of call—it's just a little less convenient. If you plan to mail anything from Castaway Cay, do so early in the day. The closer it gets to 3:30 P.M., the longer the stamp line gets.

Money Matters

There is no real need for cash on the ship. When you check in, an imprint of your credit card will be taken. (Among the cards accepted are American Express, Visa, MasterCard, the JCB Card, Discover, and Diners Club.) From then on, all you'll need to do is sign for extras you want (including excursions booked on the ship), and these amounts will be charged to that card.

SHIPBOARD AMENITIES

Here's a rundown of some of the less obvious amenities provided by Disney Cruise Line. (Charges apply.)

- ⚓ Complete laundry, dry cleaning, and valet services
- ⚓ Photo center that processes photos in an hour and has camera and video recorder rentals
- ⚓ Self-service launderettes
- ⚓ Satellite telephone services
- ⚓ Internet cafe
- ⚓ Wireless Internet service (available in many public spaces. BYO laptop.)
- ⚓ Modern medical facilities with a doctor and nurse on call
- ⚓ Stroller rentals
- ⚓ Telefax and secretarial services (on request)
- ⚓ Conference facilities for groups of up to 120

Cash or credit cards will be necessary for meals, taxis, and other purchases made in all ports except for Castaway Cay, as well as for postage at Castaway Cay. A few hundred dollars should suffice. (See page 149.) Gratuities may be pre-paid, charged to a stateroom or presented as cash placed in special envelopes. (See page 41 for tips on tipping.)

ATMs may be available in ports of call, but there are none on the ship. Before using one, make sure it dispenses U.S. currency.

Smoking

The *Disney Magic* and *Wonder* are, for the most part, smoke-free zones. All staterooms and restaurants are entirely nonsmoking. Some spots in selected lounges, on port side open-air decks and stateroom verandas, may be designated as smoking areas.

Telephone Calls

All staterooms have phones with ship-to-shore capability. Rates range from about $7–$9.50 per minute (subject to change). Toll-free and collect calls can't be placed from ship phones. Wireless service is available in staterooms. Be sure to check with your wireless carrier for rates. (See "How to Call the Ship" on page 38.) Some ports have pay phones. Use an international calling card.

Tipping

Some servers, such as bartenders and room service attendants, get an automatic 15 percent gratuity each time you call upon their services. Leave more if you deem the service to be outstanding. That said, folks such as your dining room servers and stateroom host or hostess do not receive any automatic gratuity. You have the option of pre-paying when you reserve your cruise (this helps expedite matters when the cruise comes to a close), or providing gratuities at the end of your trip. What follows is a guideline as to how much you should give to whom:

PER GUEST/ PER CRUISE	3-NIGHT	4-NIGHT	7-NIGHT
Dining Room Server	$11	$14.75	$25.25
Dining Room Assistant Server	$8	$10.75	$18.75
Dining Room Head Server	$2.75	$3.75	$6.50
Stateroom Host/Hostess	$10.75	$14.50	$25.25

If a server goes above and beyond, you may add a bit more. Conversely, if he or she doesn't live up to expectations, you may reduce the amount (this situation has never happened to us). You can charge gratuities to the stateroom (at Guest Services) or pay with cash. Envelopes and receipts are provided. Hand envelopes to their respective recipients on the last night of your trip.

ALL ABOARD

The moment you cross the gangway, you'll realize this vessel is no ordinary home away from home. Step into the grand, three-story atrium, and amidst the happy hubbub your presence is made known in dramatic fashion—with a heartfelt announcement for all to hear. And so begins your high seas adventure.

The *Disney Magic* and the *Disney Wonder* rank among the world's finest oceangoing vessels. The 2,700-passenger ships are casually elegant and designed to capture the majesty of early ocean liners. They're equipped to satisfy most cruisers, with a mix of traditional seafaring diversions and classic Disney touches. Though some theming and entertainment vary from ship to ship, the accommodations and amenities are identical. As is the service, which is expertly provided by a cast of thousands (representing dozens of countries from around the world). All 877 staterooms aboard both ships are a cut above normal cruising quarters —with an average of 25 percent more space than industry standard. The ships were designed to lure families and grown-ups without offspring to entirely different recreational areas. So, cast aside any precon-ceived notions you may have about cruising, and expect the unexpected. And don't forget to bring a camera!

Checking In

No matter where they began their journey—be it Bangkok or Boca, all Bahamas- and Caribbean-bound guests check in at Port Canaveral Terminal 8. (The check-in counter is to the left as one enters the terminal lobby.) U.S. and Canadian citizens and ARC cardholders go through the U.S. line. All others should proceed to the non-U.S. check-in area.

Though no one may board the ship until 1 P.M., guests are welcome to arrive as early as 10:30 A.M. The terminal has restrooms and ample seating to relax in while waiting to board. There's also a nifty model of the ship to give you a preview of the real thing. And, if little ones get antsy, there's lots of room for them to roam around, plus TVs that run continuous loops of Disney cartoons. Mickey Mouse and friends occasionally greet guests in the terminal, too.

Okay, we may have gotten ahead of ourselves. Before you can enter the main part of the terminal, all members of your party must go through a security checkpoint. It's a lot like airport security, so save the holey socks for the second day of your trip (you may be asked to remove your shoes, along with jackets, glasses, belts, etc.). Since kids must go through the security check, too, we recommend having snacks and games to entertain them while you wait (the line can get quite long). Once you've cleared security, head toward the escalator directly ahead. (There is an elevator, too.) You will be delivered to within steps of the check-in counter.

At the counter, you will be asked to present proper documentation for yourself and each member of your party (see page 23). This is also when you'll be asked for all of your completed

cruise paperwork (which can also be done via the Internet at *www.disneycruise.com*, under the "My Online Check-in" section (be sure to print the forms and bring them with you) and a major credit card. This card will be the one to which all of your extra cruise expenses are charged. If you'd like to split expenses with another guest staying in your stateroom, it is possible to register two different credit cards. Once the cruise begins, you'll use

your stateroom key—aka Key to the World—card, to make purchases and to open your stateroom door and safe. The card also serves as ID for debarking and reboarding purposes. Without it, you can't do either. If you'd prefer that any member of your party not have charging privileges, advise a representative at check-in (or indicate your preference when you check in online).

Once the check-in process is complete, take a peek at your watch. Is it before 1 P.M.? If so, you can settle into a seat, get a jump on the novel you plan to read poolside, or apply that first layer of sunscreen. You could also use the time to register kids for shipboard youth activities. If it's after 1 P.M., grab the kids and your day bags and head for that Mouse-shaped portal in the back of the terminal. All aboard!

HOT TIP

The midship elevators are the most crowded throughout the day, but especially at mealtimes. Try to use the forward and aft elevators whenever possible.

AHOY, MATEY!

Throughout the cruise, you may hear a few terms with which you're unfamiliar. To avoid confusion, here's a little nautical talk 101:

Aft—directional term meaning toward the back (stern) of a ship

Bow—the front of a ship

Bridge—the place from which the captain and helmsman navigate a ship and give orders

Buoy—a floating object used to mark a channel or something lying under the water

Deck—a platform stretching along a ship

Forward—a directional term meaning toward the front of a ship

Funnel—a large, hollow tube or pipe through which exhaust from a ship's engine can escape

Galley—the kitchen on a ship

Hull—the outer frame or body of a ship

Knot—the measure of a ship's speed. One knot is one nautical mile per hour.

Midship—referring to the area in the middle of a ship

Port—the left-hand side of a ship (facing forward)

Porthole—a window in the side of a ship

Starboard—the right-hand side of a ship (facing forward)

Stateroom—living quarters for passengers and crew onboard a ship (aka cabin)

Stern—the rear end of a ship

47

The Boarding Experience

After you slip through the Mickey portal, you'll enter a subdued hallway. This is where you may have your "pre-cruise" family photo taken. Try to look as stressed out and haggard as possible. That'll make the "post-cruise" shots that much more enjoyable. (You can buy the photo at Shutters.)

On the far side of the photo-op area, there's a door leading to a covered gangway. Cross that and you'll find yourself deposited smack-dab in the middle of the ship's grand lobby. A dramatic backdrop for a dramatic entrance.

Depending on the time (staterooms are usually ready at 1:30 P.M.) and your level of starvation, you may want to make a quick stateroom stop, change, and head to Parrot Cay or Topsiders (on the *Magic*) or Beach Blanket Buffet (on the *Wonder*) for lunch. The pools are usually open throughout the afternoon. If you arrive as the time nears 2:30 P.M., skip the

stateroom stop and make a beeline for the buffet—it usually closes at 3:30 P.M. After 3:30 P.M., a visit to the stateroom is imperative, as the safety drill is at 4 P.M. (For more on the drill, see page 61.)

After the safety drill, you'll head back to your room to replace the life vests and prepare for the 5 P.M. "Adventures Away" Sail Away Celebration. If you've got an early dinner seating, this is the time to change into your evening attire.

Finally, we simply cannot overemphasize the importance of making reservations for the Vista Spa & Salon and for Palo (adults-only restaurant) as early as possible. (It's best to book before the trip, via *www.disneycruise.com*.) Make last-minute spa appointments at the spa itself. For Palo, which begins accepting reservations at 1 P.M. on day one of the cruise, head for Rockin' Bar D (*Magic*) or WaveBands (*Wonder*). Plan to register children for youth activities at the Oceaneer Club and Lab in the terminal or soon after boarding (see pages 87–88 for details). It is also possible to make reservations for these activities *before* the cruise by visiting *www.disneycruise.com*.

Ship Shape

The *Disney Magic* and *Wonder* are equipped to satisfy even the most savvy of cruisers, with a mix of traditional seafaring diversions and unmistakable Disney touches. The ships'

HOT TIP

If you or a member of your party misplaces a Key to the World card while onboard, head to the Guest Services desk on Deck 3. They can issue a new one (free of charge).

classic exteriors recall the majesty of early ocean liners. Guests enter a three-story atrium, where traditional definitions of elegance expand to include bronze character statues and subtle cutout character silhouettes along a grand staircase. Recreation areas are designed to draw families and kid-free adults to different parts of the ship. By day, fun in the sun alternates with touring, lunch, indoor distractions, and perhaps even a little bingo action. Evenings give way to sunset sail-away celebrations, ultra-themed dining experiences, and theatrical extravaganzas. What follows is a description of the ships' accommodations, shops, restaurants, lounges, pools, entertainment, and more.

Decked Out

Here's the deck-by-deck rundown, from top to bottom (it covers both ships):

Deck 11

On the *Wonder*, you'll find the teen club Aloft. On the *Magic*, it's home to The Stack, also a teens-only spot (see page 73).

Deck 10

The Wide World of Sports Deck. We find it a perfect late-night place to watch the moon and stars. There's also a basketball court. And this is one of the best places to be during the sail-away party. (For more on Wide World of Sports, see page 96.) Palo is here, too. For adults only, this dining place offers fine cuisine and panoramic views.

Deck 9

Pampering, Disney style, can be enjoyed in the 10,700-square-foot Vista Spa and Salon. At the spa, guests may experience a variety of soothing treatments in the new spa villas, as well as a little

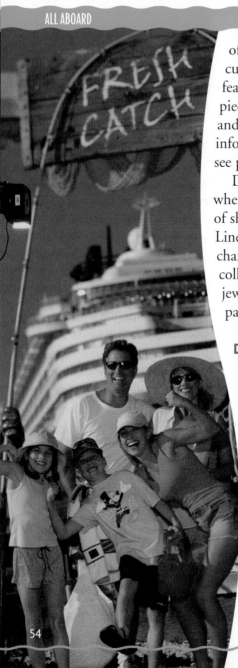

offers creatively prepared cuisine in a room that features a colorful master-piece of synchronized light and sound. (For additional information on this venue, see page 64.)

Deck 4 is also the place where you can find a couple of shops selling Disney Cruise Line–themed clothing, character merchandise, collectibles, specialty items, jewelry, and sundries. (See page 94 for more details.)

Deck 3

This is the place for dining and dancing: there's Beat Street (on the *Magic*) and Route 66 (on the *Wonder*), adult-oriented evening entertainment districts that offer themed clubs (see page 77 for details). Rockin' Bar D (on the *Magic*) has live bands performing rock 'n' roll, Top 40, and country music—and don't forget

the room's biggest attraction . . . bingo! Diversions is a sports bar; Radar Trap (on the *Wonder*) and Up Beat (on the *Magic*) are duty-free shops; Sessions (on the *Magic*) and Cadillac Lounge (on the *Wonder*) are casual yet sophisticated places to relax and listen to live piano music; and Promenade Lounge is a place to enjoy a drink and enjoy music (on both ships). Adjacent to the Promenade Lounge is the Internet Cafe. Also here is Parrot Cay (on both ships), an island-inspired restaurant serving tropical cuisine, and off the lobby is Lumière's, serving continental cuisine (on the *Magic)*. Lumière's has a French flair and a beautiful mural of Disney's *Beauty and the Beast*. Its counterpart on the *Wonder*, Triton's, has an underwater-like setting of blues, greens, and purples. With the exception of Palo, these two are the

most formal of the dining rooms onboard. Guest Services is also on this deck—it's open 24 hours a day. The Shore Excursions desk is nearby.

Deck 2

Both ships have staterooms on this deck. The *Magic* also

GUEST SERVICES DESK

As much as we like to think this book has all the answers, chances are questions will arise onboard. If so, head to the Guest Services Desk (Deck 3, midship). This is also the spot to go to secure extra copies of the *Personal Navigator* and color-coded luggage tags (for use on the last day of the cruise). Should you have any type of problem while onboard, bring it to their attention. More often than not, they will resolve the issue in a matter of minutes.

has a special area: Ocean Quest. It has a scaled down replica of the ship's bridge, complete with "windows" (an LED screen), that lets youngsters experience the view from the real bridge. It's also got a captain's chair and a simulation game that lets kids steer the ship.

Deck 1

This is where you will find the ship's Medical Center. There are some staterooms here, too.

Decks 1, 2, 5, 6, 7, and 8

Shipboard accommodations are spread over these decks.

HOT TIP

All rooms have small safes (big enough for a wallet or two, but not a laptop). There is no charge. (Lock it with a stateroom key, and unlock it using the same key.)

Staterooms

Also known as cabins, the accommodations range from standard inside rooms to suites with verandas. All 877 staterooms aboard each ship are a cut above the standard cruising cabin. On average, these staterooms offer about 25 percent more space, most have a bath and a half, and 73 percent are outside rooms with ocean vistas— many with verandas.

Cabins are decorated in a nautical theme with natural woods and imported tiles. Universal amenities include a TV, telephone with voice mail (and ship-to-shore capability), an in-room safe, a room service menu (in the Directory of Services book), and lots of drawer space. There's also a "cooling box." (It's chilly enough to store most perishables, but not medication.) After that, different types of accom- modations—which are labeled by category—offer different amenities (verandas are included in measurement of square footage):

CATEGORIES 11 AND 12

Standard inside staterooms. They have a queen or two twin beds, a single convertible sofa, a privacy divider and a bath. Each stateroom measures 184 square feet and sleeps up to 3 (category 12) or 4 (category 11).

CATEGORY 10

Deluxe inside staterooms. These accommodations are similar to those in categories 11 and 12, but have 214 square feet of space and a split bath.

CATEGORIES 8 AND 9

Deluxe ocean-view staterooms. These come with a queen or two twin beds, a single convertible sofa, a privacy divider, and split bath. The

WHAT'S A SPLIT BATH?

In staterooms ranging from category 4 through 10, accommodations come with a "split" bathroom. It's really like having two small bathrooms, side by side. One has a sink and a toilet. The other has a sink and a tub/shower.

room is 214 square feet. It sleeps up to 3 or 4.

CATEGORIES 5, 6, AND 7

Deluxe staterooms with veranda. Each has one queen or two twin-size beds, a single convertible sofa, a privacy divider, split bath, and a veranda. These rooms are 268 square feet (including the veranda) and sleep up to 4. (Category 7 has an enclosed "Navigator's Veranda," a private balcony with nautical touches. The verandas in 5 and 6 are open (with the exception of rooms in the aft area). Accommodations are otherwise the same.

CATEGORY 4

Deluxe family staterooms. This room type has a queen or two twin beds, a single convertible sofa, and a bed that pulls down from the wall. There is a privacy divider, split bath, and open veranda (verandas in the aft area are not open). It covers 304 square feet (including veranda) and sleeps up to 5.

CATEGORY 3

One-bedroom suites. These have a queen bed, an area with a double convertible sofa, and a pull-down bed (from the wall), two full baths, walk-in closet, un-stocked wet bar, DVD player, open veranda (with the exception of aft-area staterooms), and concierge service. The suite is 614 square feet (including the veranda) and sleeps up to 4 or 5.

CATEGORY 2*

Two-bedroom suites with veranda. Comes with a queen bed, a sleeper-sofa, and a pull-down bed. There are 2.5 baths, a whirlpool tub, walk-in closets, a DVD player, un-stocked wet bar, private veranda, and concierge service. The suite measures 945 square feet and sleeps up to 7.

CATEGORY 1*

Royal suite with veranda. Comes with a queen bed in one bedroom, two twin beds (in a second bedroom), and two ceiling pull-down upper berths. There are 2.5 baths, a

HOT TIP

If your formula for a restful night's sleep calls for a feather pillow, request one when you get to your stateroom. The supply is limited.

whirlpool tub in the
master bedroom, a living
room, media library (with
a pull-down bed), dining
salon, pantry, un-stocked
wet bar, walk-in closets,
DVD player, private
veranda, and concierge
service. The suite measures
1,029 square feet and
sleeps up to 7.

*If there are more than 5 guests
staying in a category 1 or 2 suite
and the accommodation is part of
a Land and Sea Vacation (cruise
paired with a stay at a comparable
Walt Disney World resort hotel),
an additional Walt Disney World
resort room will have to be booked
at an extra cost.*

The Personal Navigator

There is so much to see and
do on a daily basis, a
passenger could easily
become overwhelmed, if not
downright discombob-
ulated. Not to worry. An in-
house publication called the

CHANNEL SURFING

Each Disney ship carries up to 21
different television stations. Rather
than chastise you for watching TV
when there's about a million better
things to do onboard, here's a listing
of the channels you can expect to
find (some are commercial, some
strictly in-house). Note that all
channels are subject to blackouts:

10 Entertainment Guide
11 View from the Bridge
12 Bridge Report
13 Voyage Map
14 Shopping Channel
15 Slide/Discovery Travel
16 What's Afloat
17 Port Adventures/Debark Info
18 ABC/Discovery Channel
19 CNN Headline News
20 CNN
21 Slide/ESPN International
22 ESPN
23 ESPN 2
24 Disney Channel
25 Toon Disney
26 Music Video Channel
27 Shows from the Walt
   Disney Theatre
28 Company Clips
29 Disney Vacation Club
30 Sitcoms
31–36 Movies
37–38 Disney Animated Features

LAUNDRY FACILITIES

Laundry and dry-cleaning services are available for a fee. Items will be picked up and delivered to your stateroom. If you'd rather go the self-service laundry route, you can do so in one of several Guest Laundry Rooms. Here you'll find washers, dryers, and ironing equipment. (Due to safety concerns, the laundry room is the only place in which iron use is permitted.) There is no fee to use the iron. Machines are coin-operated and run about a buck a load. Laundry detergent may be purchased here, too. At press time, a small box cost $1. Change machines can break 1-, 5-, 10-, and 20-dollar U.S. bills.

HOT TIP

Every day brings with it a new "drink of the day." It's a specialty cocktail served at the bars and lounges onboard. The beverage will be noted in the *Personal Navigator*. It is often available at a special price.

Personal Navigator will help you make the most of every day. Updated daily and delivered to all staterooms, the publication is a comprehensive listing of the day's onboard activities, events, and entertainment.

We simply cannot overemphasize the importance of the daily *Personal Navigator*. It is a truly indispensable tool. When you get your hands on it (the first one should be waiting for you in your stateroom), drop everything and read it cover to cover. In addition to listing the lineup of activities scheduled for the rest of the day (which on day one will include the "Adventures Away" Sail Away Party), it'll provide many other handy bits of information. For instance, in the upper-right corner of the front page, you'll find the suggested evening attire

(Continued on page 62)

DAY ONE SAFETY DRILL

It's nearly 4 P.M. You've just started to unpack. You're weary from your journey. And all you want to do is plop down on a poolside lounge chair. Hold that thought. Before you get started on that much needed R & R, you've got a job to do. A very important, attendance-mandatory, skip-it-and-you've-broken-the-law job. It's called an Assembly Drill, and maritime law requires that all passengers participate prior to leaving Port Canaveral.

The drill is meant to prepare you for the unlikely event that you'd have to board a lifeboat. It sounds simple enough: Don your life jacket in your stateroom (they're on the top shelf of the stateroom closet and come in adult, child, and infant sizes), follow the signs to your assembly area, listen closely to the safety instructions, and shout out, "here!" when your stateroom number is called. But, believe it or not, some folks tend to wrestle with that life jacket for quite some time before figuring out just how to get that perfect, snug fit. And we don't want to tell you how lost we got on our way to our assembly station. That said, you might want to do a practice run. This way, when roll is called, your room can get checked off right away—and you won't have to postpone fun any longer than absolutely necessary.

Once the drill is completed (figure about 20 minutes), head directly back to your cabin to place your life jacket in its proper storage spot. Do not remove the jacket before you get to your room (though you will be tempted). Why? The straps on the jacket tend to wreak havoc with the pedestrian traffic on the stairs (the elevators do not operate during the drill). So, keep that jacket on—or risk a 50-passenger pileup.

FYI: The Disney Cruise Line safety drill has been rated number one by the United States Power Squadrons, a nonprofit organization dedicated to making boating as safe as possible. Good to know!

(Continued from page 60)

for that day. It changes from day to day, so be sure to note it. It also notes the time and location of Disney character appearances, any points of interest the ship may have scheduled, a notification of any time zone changes, as well as any "special offers" at shops or lounges. Keep an eye out for Internet discounts, too. From this pamphlet, you'll also glean the times of sunrise and sunset, should you aspire to be on an observation deck for Mother Nature's daily presentations.

Dining

A Disney cruise is not the place to count calories—although, if you must, there are fat-free, low-carb, and low-calorie menu options. There's no shortage of rations on these ships. If your tastes are simple (say, a hot dog at Pluto's Dog House) or sublime (how does a juicy filet mignon,

A TENDER SUBJECT

Some ports require a process called "tendering." This means, rather than pulling right up to a dock, the ship will pull close to port and drop anchor. Ferries take guests back and forth to shore. It's an efficient system, but it could knock you for a loop if you're not expecting it—especially if you've got an early excursion booked. In this case, you'll have to leave a whole lot earlier than you originally planned.

If the ship will be tendered at St. Thomas after leaving a foreign port, expect a 7 A.M. visit from U.S. Immigration. Attendance is mandatory. (Currently, St. Thomas is the only port of call where guests must present themselves to customs.)

courtesy of Palo, sound?), rest assured you'll never be hungry. Or understimulated, for that matter, as many of the restaurants are down-right entertaining. And, thanks to a system called "rotational dining," you'll have a chance to experience three restaurants, all the while being made to feel like a VIP by your serving staff. That means you'll eat at a different one of the three main restaurants each evening, often with the same table guests, and enjoy the services of the same waitstaff. Your serving team gets to know you, as well as your likes and dislikes, very well. The system, which is unique to Disney Cruise Line, tends to get the thumbs-up from cruise veterans and newcomers alike. The only exception to the rule is Palo, the adults-only, advance reservations-necessary restaurant. (For details on Palo, see page 68.)

How do you know where to go on which night? Easy. A ticket with all the details will be waiting for you in your stateroom. The details are also printed on your Key to the World card. Don't forget to check the day's *Personal Navigator* to note the style of dress for the evening.

Table Service

Each Disney ship has four table-service restaurants, three of which are included in the unique "rotational dining" system. They all serve dinner, but check the

Personal Navigator for hours and meals served at each spot for the rest of the day.

Animator's Palate

The *pièce de résistance*—as far as Disney creativity goes—is without a doubt Animator's Palate, a place where diners not only have to decide what to eat, but what to watch! Simple surprises abound at each stage of the evening meal.

Upon entering the all black-and-white dining room, you will be led to your table and asked for your order. Note the soft background music and the black-and-white sketches along the wall. While you're doing so, drinks and appetizers will be served. If you ignore this distraction and keep your gaze fixed on the walls, you may notice a bit of color creeping into that sketch of Cinderella. By the time the entrées make their entrance, the room is ablaze in living color. The music tends to get a bit livelier by this point, too. You may even notice that your waitstaff becomes more colorful toward meal's end. The menu features items such as grilled salmon, filet mignon, and other tempting choices. If they're available, we recommend starting with the butternut squash soup and capping it off with a slice of double-fudge chocolate cake. The ice cream is rather tasty, too.

The experience at Animator's Palate is the same on both the *Magic* and the *Wonder*.

Lumière's

Located on the *Magic* only, this elegant spot provides fine dining in a setting inspired by *Beauty and the Beast*. The sprawling dining room is elegant and softly

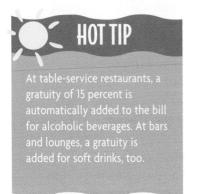

lit, though a bit more raucous than its cosmopolitan contemporaries (see the photo on page 65). Note that the later seating is a tad more sedate.

Menu selections at dinner have included smoked duck breast with cabbage pie and garlic-roasted beef tenderloin. Vegetarians can opt for the rigatoni pasta Provencal. And waist-watchers won't feel cheated by the baked salmon steak. For dessert, consider the crème brûlée or crepes suzette. Sugar-free selections are available, too: chocolate mousse and an apple-cinnamon fruit dish served with a brownie.

Triton's

Passengers aboard the *Wonder* may dine in the elegant Triton's, where the specialty of the house is seafood. (It is, after all, named for the Little Mermaid's dad, King Triton.) The ocean theme is enhanced by subtly changing lighting with every course, the room getting greener and greener as the meal progresses. Menu items include the shrimp medley, bouillabaisse, and duck fricassee. For dessert, there's cherries jubilee, Montelimar frozen nougat, and more.

Parrot Cay

This tropical spot, which is located on both ships and is pronounced Parrot *KEY*, is certainly one of the most whimsical spaces you'll ever dine in. Done up in vibrant shades of orange, green, blue, and yellow, it boasts a rainbow of cleverly formed napkin displays at each table. The island-like feel is complemented by such dinner dishes as beef tenderloin, barbecued pork with prickly pear glaze, grilled shrimp, lamb chop, and grilled sausage. Kids

appreciate the fact that the menu also includes macaroni and cheese, a Disney specialty. Dessert-wise, expect the likes of lemon meringue pie with kumquat sauce, and chocolate-espresso walnut cake.

HOT TIP

Palo reservations will not appear on your *Personal Navigator*. (It's not *that* personal!) Make sure you don't miss it. There is a $15 per person charge for brunch and dinner, and $5 for high tea—show or no-show.

Palo

For adults only, Palo is an ideal spot for special celebrations or just a quiet, romantic evening. Offering brunch, dinner, and high tea (during 7-night or longer

cruises), it's worth the small surcharge (at press time, prices were $15 for brunch and dinner; $5 for high tea) to indulge in a five-star dining experience that includes an ocean view.

True to its name (*palo* means "pole" in Italian), the restaurant has echoes of Venice, Italy. Masks from that city's Carnivale line the walls, and the menu reflects some of the best continental fare you'll find this side of the Atlantic. For dinner, appetizers include fresh, homemade (and delicious) pizzas and classic Caesar salads with thinly sliced Parmesan cheese. The entrée menu tempts with selections such as penne *arrabiata* with grilled shrimp, grilled lamb chops with mushroom risotto, and lobster over asparagus risotto. (Your server will take the lobster out of the shell for you.) A warning: Save room for dessert or you'll never forgive yourself. The chocolate soufflé (with hot chocolate and vanilla sauces) is beyond amazing. (The soufflé must be ordered in advance.) The pistachio tart with ice cream and berries yields raves, too.

Brunch at Palo is indeed a special event. (It's available on all cruises that are 4 days or longer.) The buffet is so vast that it requires a guided tour (which, happily, you will receive). Expect to sample fruit, pastries, salads, seafood, made-to-order omelets, fish, and chicken entrées, and more. Once again, dessert is a must.

High tea, served at 3:30 P.M. and 4:30 P.M. exclusively on 7-night cruises, is another way to sample the delights here. A variety of teas is available. Nibbles include finger sandwiches, cookies, cakes, warm scones served with thick cream and jam, as well as other treats.

Palo is for diners age 18 years and older. Reservations are required and can be made at *www.disneycruise.com,* or at Rockin' Bar D (*Magic*) or WaveBands (*Wonder*) starting at about 1 P.M. on the first day of a cruise.

NOTE: *Palo has brunch during 4- and 7-night-or-longer cruises. High tea is offered on 7-night cruises only. Shorts, jeans, bathing suits, and tank tops are not acceptable attire for any meal at Palo.*

Seating Times and Situations

There are two seating sessions for dinner: The first has seating times of 5:30 P.M., 5:45 P.M., and 6 P.M. The second has seating times of 8 P.M., 8:15 P.M., and 8:30 P.M. If you have a preference, be sure to tell your travel agent or reservationist the moment you book your cruise. However, requests for any seating cannot be guaranteed. If you get closed out of a particular seating time, check with Guest Services after boarding. Sometimes folks switch plans after arrival. Most of the seating at table-service restaurants is communal (with the exception of Palo). If you are traveling as a family with kids, expect to be seated with the same. Adults without kids will be seated together when possible.

What to Wear for Dinner
The attire for Animator's Palate and Parrot Cay is casual. Lumière's, Triton's, and Palo are more formal. On select nights, there will be a theme: tropical, pirate attire, semi-formal, etc. On such days, the desired style of dress will be noted in the *Personal Navigator*. Generally speaking, "cruise casual" is the way to go: collared shirts, blouses, cotton pants, jeans, and sundresses are generally acceptable for evenings in the restaurants—shorts, swimsuits, T-shirts, and tank tops are not.

Wine and Dine
Each of the table-service restaurants (including Palo) offers many vintages by the glass or by the bottle. If you order a bottle and fail to finish it by meal's end, ask your server to store it for you.

(You will get it with your next evening's meal.)

For guests who expect to enjoy more than a bottle over the course of the cruise, Disney offers two wine packages (both include red and white selections).

Special Dietary Needs

Many special dietary needs, such as low-sodium, low-carb, lactose-free, or kosher meals, may be met aboard Disney cruise ships. All requests should be made well in advance, preferably at the time of booking. It's always a good idea to confirm the request prior to setting sail.

SELF-SERVE, FAST FOOD, AND SNACKS

Topsider's Buffet and Beach Blanket Buffet

Located on the *Magic* and *Wonder*, respectively, these self-service buffets offer breakfast and lunch. The morning meal brings selections such as fresh fruit,

cereal, eggs, sausage, oatmeal, etc. Lunch fare usually has a theme: Italian, Chinese, seafood, etc. (Check a *Personal Navigator*, or at the restaurant itself, to learn if there's a theme for the meal.) In addition to the buffet (which you will encounter as you enter the restaurant), there is also a serving station by the seating area. This area serves omelets in the morning, and usually has something special for lunch. There are indoor tables and others out on the deck. Note that Topsider's (on the *Magic*) offers table service and casual dining for dinner.

FUN FOOD FACTS

Apparently, cruising makes passengers exceptionally hungry. Here's what's put away on an average 7-night voyage on the *Disney Magic*.

⚓ Rib-eye steak—800 to 1,000 pounds

⚓ Beef strip loin—2,000 pounds

⚓ Beef tenderloin—2,500 pounds

⚓ Whole chickens—9,000 pounds

⚓ Fresh salmon—900 pounds

⚓ Grouper—300 pounds

⚓ Shrimp—2,200 pounds

⚓ Lobster tail—900 pounds

⚓ Fresh melon—10,500 pounds

⚓ Fresh pineapple—4,400 pounds

⚓ Yogurt—2,400 tubs

⚓ Cereal—7,920 packets

⚓ Individual eggs—44,500

⚓ Tomato ketchup—26,000 packets

⚓ Mayonnaise—15,000 packets

⚓ Sugar—40,000 packets

⚓ Beer—7,100 bottles/cans

⚓ Wine and champagne—2,200 bottles

Beverage Station

There is a self-serve station on Deck 9 by the Mickey pool. Feel free to help yourself to water, juice, soda, lemonade, iced tea, coffee, hot chocolate, and hot tea. There is an ice machine, too. The station is generally open 24 hours a day, though not all selections are available at all times. (If the machine fails to dispense ice, get room service delivery.) Note that carbonated soft drinks are free here (there used to be a charge for anything fizzy) and with meals, but not at bars and lounges or through room service (where they carry a charge).

HOT TIP

Children's menus are available in all shipboard restaurants (with the obvious exception of Palo). Buffets all stock kid-friendly vittles such as mac and cheese and chicken nuggets.

Aloft and The Stack

These teen-only spots have a selection of (non-alcoholic) smoothie drinks, as well as snacks and other soft drinks. There are MP3 listening stations, plus lots of games and magazines. Aloft is exclusive to the *Disney Wonder*. There is an extra charge for the refreshments here. (The teens-only equiva-lent on the *Magic* is The Stack. It provides a similar experience and atmosphere.)

Cove Cafe

A cozy, adults-only lounge, Cove Cafe can be found aboard both ships. It features espresso and other specialty coffees and a full bar. Cakes and cookies are available, too. Be aware that there is an extra charge to indulge in snacks and beverages here.

Books and magazines are available for complimentary on-site perusing. Board games may be borrowed, too. There are several laptop computers available to borrow. This is usually an excellent alternative to the Internet Cafe, as it's much less trafficked. There is a charge for Internet access. The cafe is adjacent to Signals bar, near the Quiet Cove Pool.

Pinocchio's Pizzeria

A counter-service spot serving spirits and soft drinks (for a fee) and cheese and pepperoni pizzas. There is often a special pizza of the day. Be sure to ask.

Pluto's Dog House

Located at the foot of Mickey's Pool, this window serves hot dogs, bratwurst, hamburgers, veggie burgers, fish burgers, grilled chicken sandwiches, tacos, and chicken tenders.

Goofy's Galley

A popular snack spot, this counter specializes in ice cream and frozen yogurt. It also dispenses salads, wraps, panini sandwiches, cookies, and fresh fruit. The selection tends to change throughout the day, so it pays to check back from time to time.

ROOM SERVICE

Stateroom dining service delivers 24 hours a day—very handy if you're traveling with children or if you have a serious snack craving in between meals. Most menu items are included with your cruise package. At press time, selections included soups, salads, sandwiches, burgers, pizza, cookies, and selections for kids. There is a charge for beverages and certain snack selections (such as candy, popcorn, wine, beer, soda, and water). Gratuity isn't always included.

SPECIAL DINING EXPERIENCES

Character Breakfast

An up-close-and-personal morning starring furry favorites is a very Disney way to start the day. (This is available on cruises of seven nights or longer.) Check your Dining Ticket for assigned mornings. Everyone gets to attend at least one character breakfast per cruise. Characters vary. Be sure to bring your camera. Characters have been known to dance with younger guests, too.

Held at Parrot Cay, many of the character breakfast selections remain staples—eggs, cereal, and Mickey Mouse French toast, for example.

Till We Meet Again Dinner

Presented on the final evening of 7-night cruises, this meal is an opportunity to enjoy new favorite dishes, celebrate new friends, and perhaps even start planning (or at least dreaming about) your next cruise. Menu items include Nori-wrapped salmon and roasted-mint-pesto-crusted lamb.

Captain's Gala Dinner

Even on this, one of the planet's most casual of cruises, there is a chance to don your finery and join the sparkle and glitter of this black-tie (optional) affair. If you'd rather not get completely decked out, go with a business casual look (but not too casual). The same French-continental menu will be offered in each of the main dining rooms. The Captain's Gala is offered on 7-night cruises only.

Pirates IN the Caribbean Party

If there's one thing Disney really knows how to do right, it's throw a party. On one night during every

HOT TIP

You may bring your own (unopened) bottle of wine to dinner. A $15 corking fee will be charged to your shipboard account for each bottle that was not purchased onboard.

cruise, guests enjoy dinner while wearing special bandanas. (If you happen to own any pirate attire or regalia, be sure to don it for the big event.) After the meal, everyone heads up to Decks 9 and 10, where Captain Hook and Mr. Smee set their sights on taking over the ship. An epic battle ensues as the good guys take on the villains. The greatest spectacle of all is the grand finale—a fireworks display! It's the only one of its kind done at sea.

Family Tea

An afternoon tea party with one of Disney's beloved characters is a true kid-pleaser. A relaxing break in the day's activities, the party host will gladly sign autographs and pose for pictures. The tea is held at Studio Sea. Reservations are necessary and may be made at Guest Services. It is offered on 7-night cruises. There is no extra charge.

Bars and Lounges

From elegant spots with live piano music to rousing sports bars, the Disney ships have a bounty of bars and lounges in which to wet your whistle or simply unwind and watch the waves or the sunset.

Signals

Located on Deck 9, this poolside spot serves spirits (including the daily drink special) and soft drinks.

Cadillac Lounge

Unique to Route 66 (*Wonder*), this sophisticated spot celebrates classic cars and soothing music.

Cove Cafe

On both the *Wonder* and the *Magic*, this adults-only coffee bar also serves beer, wine, and specialty drinks. Snacks are available, too. (There is a charge for items ordered here.) Reading material may be borrowed.

Diversions

A sports fan's dream come true, this lounge has a satellite feed (often showing more than one game at a time), plus suds and (occasionally) wings, hot dogs, and other stadium-style munchies.

Outlook Bar

Overlooking the Quiet Cove Pool (grown-ups only), this bar serves beer, wine, cocktails, and soft drinks.

Promenade Lounge

A sprawling spot with lots of seating, this laid-back lounge serves drinks throughout the day. At night, it adds live music to the mix.

Rockin' Bar D

This Beat Street joint (*Magic*) fancies itself a roadhouse honky-tonk. Expect to hear a mix of live music and deejay-selected tunes. There's a dance floor, plus tables and bar seating. Themed parties are thrown here on select nights.

Sessions

The *Magic*'s version of an intimate piano bar, this elegant lounge serves cocktails and caviar.

WaveBands

Vintage radios and classic album covers line the walls and set the stage for a

(*Continued on page 80*)

BE BORED: WE DARE YOU!

On any given day, guests aboard a Disney ship have a plethora of activities to engage in. On one of our sea days aboard the *Magic* (you can enjoy similar events on *Wonder*), we were offered the following:

10 A.M. **Team Trivia**

11 A.M. **Pool Games**

11:30 A.M. **Crab Racing**

1 P.M. **Disney Behind the Scenes** (tour of the Walt Disney Theatre)

1:30 P.M. **Character Autograph Session**

1:30 P.M. **Family Golf Putting**

2 P.M. **"Dive-In" Movie**

2 P.M. **Disney's Art of Entertaining** (cake decorating)

2 P.M. **Beer Tasting**

2:30 P.M. **Wine Tasting**

2:45 P.M. **Disney's Navigator Series** (walking tour of the ship)

3 P.M. **Pool Games**

3:30 P.M. **Mr. Toad's Wild Race**

3:30 P.M. **Jackpot Bingo**

3:30 P.M. **High Tea at Palo**

4:30 P.M. **Chip It Golf**

4:30–5:30 P.M. Family Basketball Time

4:45–5:30 P.M. Salsa Dancing

5:30–6:15 P.M. Dancing Music

5:30 P.M. Family Sing-along

5:45–6:30 P.M. Captain's Welcome Reception

5:45–6:30 P.M. Family Dance Party

6:15 P.M. The Golden Mickeys

7:30–8:30 P.M. Family Dance Party

7:30–8:30 P.M. Pin Trading

7:45–8:30 P.M. Captain's Welcome Reception

8:30 P.M. Tailgate Party

8:30 P.M. Twice Charmed—An Original Twist on the Cinderella Story

9:30–10:15 P.M. Who Wants to Be a Mouseketeer?

10:15–11:30 P.M. Family Karaoke

10:15 P.M. Cabaret Show

10:45 P.M. 70's Boogie Down Disco Night

12–2 A.M. Dance Party

Note that some events are repeated to accommodate guests dining early and those with late seatings. Some activities are for grown-ups only. These listings were taken from actual *Personal Navigators*.

(Continued from page 77)

lively dance club. A deejay keeps the place grooving till the wee hours. All manner of beverages are available at this Route 66 club (*Wonder*).

Entertainment

For some, a deck chair, a good book, and a steady stream of sunshine is all the entertainment required. Others may delight in an evening of dancing or a bingo-filled afternoon. And some are satisfied with nothing short of an all-out Broadway-style stage show. Fortunately, Disney Cruise Line has all of the above, plus guest lecturers, behind-the-scenes tours, and a whole lot more. Check the daily *Personal Navigator* for show schedules. Note that all shows are not presented every day. Keep in mind that the entertainment lineup is tweaked from time to time, so some details may differ during your cruise.

STAGE SHOWS

The majestic Walt Disney Theatre (Deck 4, forward) is the venue in which Disney Cruise Line presents a lineup of lavish Broadway-style musical performances. Among them: *Toy Story—The Musical*; *Disney Dreams—An Enchanted Classic*; *Twice Charmed—An Original Twist on the Cinderella Story*; and *The Golden Mickeys*.

This 977-seat theater, which spans five decks, also hosts variety shows, the big payoff final bingo game, and more.

The Golden Mickeys

A dynamic production that pays tribute to the musical legacy of Walt Disney Studios. It's got all the glitz and glamour of a Hollywood celebration, paying homage to the comedy, romance, and heroes (plus a few key villains) of classic Disney animated films. This show is presented on both the *Magic* and *Wonder*. It's a consistent crowd-pleaser.

All Aboard: Let the Magic Begin

This sweet presentation is a great way to "meet" your ship's crew—the captain, cruise director, and many of their comrades introduce themselves and welcome everyone aboard. Musical numbers and vaudeville-like variety acts round out the bill. This show is a Disney *Magic* exclusive.

Disney Dreams—An Enchanted Classic

This bedtime story features a galaxy of characters, including Peter Pan, Belle, Beast, Aladdin, Cinderella,

GREAT FOR GROWN-UPS

Among the most interesting of the offerings for the over-18 crowd are the special "Navigator Series" and "Behind the Scenes" presentations. Normally offered on sea days, these programs feature insight into the inner workings of the Disney ships and the creative forces behind them. On many Eastern Caribbean sailings there are guest speakers from various divisions of The Walt Disney Company who discuss their jobs and field questions from guests. From Imagineers to company historians, the lectures are quite lively and informative. You may even catch a sailing that features an author who has written about Disney—and have the opportunity to purchase a copy of the author's book and have it autographed.

DID YOU KNOW?

The anchor on the *Disney Magic* weighs 28,200 pounds—about the same as three full-grown elephants!

and Ariel. Together and through the power of song (and dance) the characters teach a skeptical girl about the power of dreams. It takes place on both ships.

Toy Story–The Musical: Fans of the beloved movie will delight as it comes to life in one of the largest productions ever developed for a cruise ship. The story isn't new—but the music is! The tunes help tell the story of Buzz, Woody, and the gang of toys from Andy's room in a fun and energizing way. It's generally a hit with kids of all ages—including those whose toybox days are long behind them. At press time, the show was a *Wonder* exclusive, but that may change in 2009.

Twice Charmed–An Original Twist on the Cinderella Story
A Broadway-style extravaganza (*Magic* only), this musical production begins with the wedding of Cinderella and Prince Charming. Things take a sudden turn when the wicked Fairy Godfather makes his presence known and, after granting a wish to one evil stepmother, sends the family back in time, where—gasp—the glass slipper gets broken! Does this destroy Cinderella's chances of living happily ever after? You'll have to catch the show to find out.

Remember the Magic: A Final Farewell
This show wraps up the trip as performers celebrate a week of shipboard activities and island-hopping. *Disney Magic* only.

DECK PARTIES

When it comes to on-deck celebrations, the area by Goofy's Pool is party central. Starting with the "Adventures Away" Sail Away Celebration and continuing with daily dance fests with Disney characters, live bands, and fireworks, it seems like there is always a reason to party. Check the *Personal Navigator* for specifics.

HOT TIP

When the weather's good, it's breezy on deck. When the weather's less than perfect, it is breezier. When the weather's bad, it's downright gusty. If you've got long hair and you intend to explore outside deck areas, bring a band or a clip to tie your hair back.

FAMILY ENTERTAINMENT

Studio Sea

A colorful "TV studio" environment is the setting for audience participation family game shows. *Mickey Mania* lets you put your knowledge of Disney trivia to the test, while *Karaoke Night* encourages families to take the stage and sing together. Finally, the *Family Dance Party* gives all members of the family a chance to kick up their heels (or sneakers) and enjoy a party for guests of all ages. Keep in mind that the entertainment line-up, though always dynamic, is subject to change.

Character Breakfast

On all cruises that are 7 nights or longer, this breakfast is hosted by familiar Disney friends at

Parrot Cay. In addition to the plentiful fare, you'll enjoy a little Breakfast Hand Jive.

Family Tea

Guests of all ages, but especially little ones (on 7-night cruises), are invited to enjoy afternoon tea with Wendy Darling or Alice and the Mad Hatter at Studio Sea. In addition to learning the proper way to serve tea and cookies, guests are treated to a story or two about their hostess's own adventures. Tickets are available at Guest Services (they're free). For more information on afternoon tea, turn to page 76.

FOR GROWN-UPS ONLY

The over-18 set on the *Magic* can attend intriguing demonstrations (i.e., Disney's Art of Entertaining), lectures and conversations with guest speakers, tours (of the ship's galley and other areas of interest), specially tailored nighttime events (such as *Match Your Mate*, a game show in which you and your mate will find out how much you know about each other), as well as theme nights, cabaret shows, and more.

JUST FOR KIDS

The kids' programs and activities tend to elicit raves from participants and parents alike. For starters, adults who leave their kids at supervised facilities can be assured that the watchword here is safety. There are 47 counselors, with a ratio of one counselor for every six children in the toddler age group, one for every 15 kids in the age 3-to-4 demographic, and one for every 25 in the 5-to-12 crowd. The secured programming allows counselors to know where every child is at any given time (kids register when entering and sign out when

HOT TIP

Looking for a little privacy? There is a little-known outdoor nook—complete with comfy chairs—on Deck 7 aft.

exiting with an authorized guardian). Records of a child's allergies or other particular needs are entered into their file. Every youngster is required to wear a wristband that identifies him or her as a participant in the program.

85

Parents get beepers and can be contacted immediately if their child has a problem or just wants to see them.

Cleanliness is a priority, too. In fact, kids entering the Oceaneer Club are promptly asked to put out their hands. After a quick squirt of liquid soap, they wash up before engaging in any of the activities. Play areas are cleaned three times a day, with a deep-down cleansing done at the end of each day.

The children's programs are divided up by age group. They are concen- trated on Deck 5, but supervised groups may leave the designated play areas. The specially tailored programming is open to all kids ages 3 through 12 who are completely potty- trained, able to interact comfortably within the counselor-to-child ratio groups, and able to interact well with peers.

A child may participate in an older age group if he or she is within one month of the minimum age for that group. If your kids simply can't bear to be separated, know that older kids may stay with their younger siblings.

Kids who exhibit symptoms of illness—even if it's just a runny nose— will not be allowed to participate. If a child becomes disruptive, he or she may not be allowed to

participate without a parent or guardian present.

Except for Flounder's Reef Nursery, there is no fee to participate in youth activities. The following descriptions of the youth activities were accurate at press time, but specifics are subject to change from time to time:

Oceaneer Club

A wonderfully detailed adventure zone, the interior of Oceaneer Club has a pirate theme. In addition to computer games, costumes, and other games, there are lots of organized activities.

Among the activities for the 3- and 4-year-olds are *Mouseketeer Training* (where children train to be Mouse-keteers by marching and watching the *Mickey Mouse Club*, etc.; the Mouse himself pops in to inspect the new crew of recruits and even leads them in a march), *Magical Adventures*

with Wendy (an adventure with music, games, and the story of Neverland, with Wendy Darling), and *Do-Si-Do with Snow White* (dancing with one of the Enchanted Forest's most famous residents).

The 5–7 set enjoys activities such as *So You Want to Be a Pirate?* (where an actual swashbuckler—a buddy of Captain Hook—tells tales of buccaneer adventures), *Gases In Action* (a funny hands-on demonstration that proves that "if it isn't solid or liquid. . . it's a gas!"), *Stitch's*

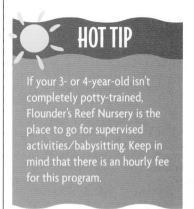

HOT TIP

If your 3- or 4-year-old isn't completely potty-trained, Flounder's Reef Nursery is the place to go for supervised activities/babysitting. Keep in mind that there is an hourly fee for this program.

Great Adventure (a program that invites youngsters to help Stitch capture ten of his lost "experiments"), and *Flubber* (where kids join a wacky professor to explore a squishy green mystery substance). Lunch and dinner are served.

Oceaneer Lab

The Lab is open to kids ages 8 through 12, with the kids divided into groups made up of 8- and 9-year-olds and another with those ages 10 through 12. The room is filled with wacky inventions and opportunities for exploration. There are music stations, games, computers,

video games, drawing materials, and more. As with the Oceaneer Club, there are also several imaginative organized activities.

Kids ages 8–9 can enjoy programs such as *Flubber* (and in doing so encounter solid liquids and mix a batch of green goop), *Quack-amation* (which unlocks some of the secrets of Disney animation), and *A Junior Chef Experience* (which lets kids help bake cookies).

Kids in the 10–12 group experience *Flubber* (where kids gain insight into the magic of science), *Animation Cell* (a class in animation technique that lets kids create their own cel), *Ship Factor* (which challenges teams in bizarre and wacky competitions), and more. Lunch and dinner are served.

Reminder: *Kids ages 8–12 may check themselves in and out of the Oceaneer Lab with their parents' permission.*

HOT TIP

The last night of every cruise features a farewell celebration in the ship's lobby. It's a chance to say thank-you and good-bye to your crew—including all the Disney characters! Don't miss it.

Ocean Quest

Kids ages 10–14 can play Captain as they steer the ship from this scaled replica of the bridge. LCD screens let kids get a simulated view from the *Magic*'s bridge. There are video games, arts and crafts, and plasma-screen TVs for movie-viewing, too. Note that Ocean Quest is unique to the *Magic*.

Flounder's Reef Nursery

Open to children ages 12 weeks through 3 years, this colorful space with an under-the-sea theme is the ship's babysitting center. It offers toddler-friendly activities and a quiet area, complete with cribs.

No food is available at Flounder's Reef, but if parents provide prepared bottles or jarred food that is clearly labeled with a child's name, staffers will happily feed their hungry tyke. Space is limited and gets booked early. In fact,

reservations are accepted via *www.disneycruise.com* and on embarkation day on a first-come, first-served basis. Due to the high demand, multiple requests may not be honored—so don't count on securing several sessions, though it can't hurt to give it a try. The fee for the babysitting service is $6 per hour for the first child, $5 per each additional child with a 2-hour minimum (siblings net the discount). *Note that in-stateroom babysitting is not available on either ship.*

TEENS ONLY

Teens can enjoy their own special hangouts and activities while aboard Disney ships. The Stack is a teen-only club on the *Magic*, while Aloft is their exclusive place to hang on the *Wonder*. Both places are open to guests ages 13 through 17 only. They've got music, games, dance

THE BIG GOOD-BYE

At the end of the cruise, kids who participated in children's programs will have the chance to be onstage at the Walt Disney Theatre and perform a song. They march in graduation ceremony style, wearing new T-shirts and mortarboard caps complete with mouse ears (that they can keep as souvenirs). Depending on the number of kids in the programs, the theater can be quite full—so arrive early for a seat with a good view.

parties, big-screen TVs, Internet access (for a fee), snacks, and more. (The activities and sodas are free, but smoothies cost extra.) Other teen-oriented programs include karaoke, organized sports activities, and a pool party.

FUN AND GAMES
Arcade
Located on Deck 9, by Goofy's family pool, Quarter Master's Arcade is a small room replete with modern electronic games and an air hockey table. You'll need to purchase credits to play.

Bingo
Perhaps it's something in the ocean air, but nothing brings out the bingo fanatic in you like a few days at sea. The closest thing to gambling that you'll find on a Disney vessel, the daily bingo tournaments are extremely popular. You have to be at least 18 to play, but kids can watch over Mom's or Dad's shoulder and cheer them on. Each session has several individual games. Boards can be purchased one at a time, or in bunches. Beware the hard-sell push to get the "grand plan." It's nearly impossible to keep

track of all those boards. There is a rolling jackpot—meaning that if no one wins the big prize each day, it rolls over to the next session. That is until the last day bingo is played. Then they call numbers until somebody wins. (On a recent cruise, a lucky guest won a $7,000 jackpot. Sadly, it wasn't us.) *Warning*: The banter of the bingo callers can become a tad cloying. Whatever you do, don't encourage them.

Games

Ping-Pong, foosball, shuffleboard, basketball . . . they're all here. Equipment

can usually be found by the tables or courts. (Don't monopolize it—it's for everyone to share.) Borrow games from Guest Services. Kooky competitions are sometimes held poolside. See a *Personal Navigator* for details.

Movies

The Buena Vista Theatre shows new releases and animated classics. This is the perfect place to head when

DISNEY CRUISE LINE GIFTS

Whether you'll be celebrating a special occasion or simply consider the cruise as a special occasion unto itself, you may want to have a gift item delivered to your stateroom as an added surprise. Among the items than can be pre-ordered by visiting *disneycruise.com* are flower arrangements, food and beverage packages, wine selections, and Disney Cruise Line merchandise. Once onboard, you can order via stateroom phone. Allow at least 24 hours for delivery.

broadcasts Disney features, popular TV shows, and sporting events at various times throughout the cruise.

SHOPPING

While onboard Disney's cruise ships, you can enjoy tax-free (on all items) and duty-free (selected items) shopping. Check the *Personal Navigator* for hours and details about special merchandise events such as pin-trading or Captain's Signing (when the captain autographs collectibles that can be purchased onboard). The shops have limited hours due to U.S. Customs regulations and can't operate during any time when the ship is in port. Use your stateroom key (Key to the World) to buy items in the ship's shops and on Castaway Cay.

the weather is less than ideal. Get there early, as the 268 seats fill up quickly. It is located on Deck 5, aft.

If you prefer your flicks alfresco, make a beeline for the Goofy Pool. A jumbo screen (affixed to the forward funnel on Deck 9 and known as Ariel Vision)

DUTY-FREE SHOPPING—RULES TO SHOP BY

If unlimited duty-free shopping sounds too good to be true, well, it is. There are limits. Federally enforced limits. The specifics vary slightly, depending on where you do your shopping. Know that the rules are mandated by U.S. law and are subject to change.

⚓ **Bahamas**—Each guest re-entering the U.S. from the Bahamas can bring up to $800 (U.S. currency) worth of duty-free treasures. Those of legal drinking age (that's 21 and up) can pick up two liters of alcohol, of which one must be produced in the Bahamas. Legal adults (that's the 18-and-over crowd) are limited to 200 cigarettes and 100 cigars (with the exception of Cuban cigars—they're illegal to bring to the U.S.).

⚓ **Eastern Caribbean**—Guests who voyage to the Eastern Caribbean and back to the U.S. can bring back up to $1,600 worth of duty-free stuff. However, no more than $800 of it can be purchased on the ship, St. Maarten, and Castaway Cay combined. The rest has to come from St. Thomas. Or, the entire $1,600 may be used toward purchases made on St. Thomas alone. Got that? If not, read it again—it's important. As for alcohol, each legal drinker is limited to five liters—only one liter can come from St. Maarten or the ship, with an additional four liters being exempt if they were purchased on St. Thomas and at least one liter of that allotment was produced in the U.S. Virgin Islands. Each guest 18 or older is limited to five cartons of cigarettes (only one carton may be purchased on St. Maarten or the ship, with an additional four cartons being exempt if purchased on St. Thomas). You're allowed 100 cigars (no Cubans).

⚓ **Western Caribbean**—If you are returning from the Western Caribbean to the U.S., you may bring up to $800 worth of duty-free booty from Grand Cayman, Cozumel, and Castaway Cay. If you're at least 21 years old, you can buy one liter of alcohol. Older than 18? You're entitled to 200 cigarettes and 100 cigars (again, don't even *think* of bringing in Cuban cigars).

ONBOARD SHOPS
Preludes

There is a snack bar–concession window on either side of the Walt Disney Theatre. It usually closes at 10 P.M., but opens at different times. Among the items for sale are cookies, candies, nuts, lollipops, and drinks.

Mickey's Mates

Located on Deck 4, forward, this retail spot offers Disney Cruise Line logo merchandise, including souvenirs, clothing, beach towels, swimwear, character costumes, gifts, postcards, mugs, and plush toys.

Treasure Ketch

Directly across the hall from Mickey's Mates on Deck 4, this shop sells tax-free watches, jewelry, loose gemstones, and limited-edition Disney collectibles. There's a selection of upscale clothing for men and women, including shirts, sweatshirts, hats, jackets, and other Disney Cruise Line logo items. Duty-free fragrances are available, too. The store also stocks batteries, disposable cameras, books, magazines, sun-care products, and a limited selection of sundries (including Dramamine). Clocks (like the ones in staterooms) can be purchased here. Be sure to ask about their special daily offers.

Up Beat and Radar Trap

Located on Deck 3, forward of the *Magic* and *Wonder*, respectively, these counter-service spots offer tax- and duty-free watches, liquor, snacks, and more. Note that any liquor purchased here may not be consumed while onboard. It will be delivered to your room on the last evening of your cruise. Everything else may be consumed (or worn) during the cruise.

SHOPS ON CASTAWAY CAY
Castaway Cay Post Office
They keep things simple here: stamps only. We recommend purchasing stamps at the beginning of the day. Cash only, please.

She Sells Seashells and Everything Else
Have to have a Castaway Cay hat, pin, or T-shirt? This is the place to get it. A mini-bazaar comprised of a hut or two and outdoor stands, "She" also sells beach toys, towels, batteries, sun-care products, tropical wear for the whole family, and, of course, collectible pins and Disney character toys. You'll also find postcards, beach attire, and more.

SPORTS AND RECREATION
Health Club
A renovated and expanded (it's twice the original size!) work-out room, the health club is located within the Vista Spa and Salon. There is no fee to use the equipment, which includes treadmills, bikes, stair-climbing machines, a huge selection of weights, and more. (Some of the equipment sport their own TVs—bring headphones or borrow a pair at the front desk.) There's an area for spinning, group instruction, and one-on-one fitness consultations. The health club, as well as the rest of the Vista Spa and Salon, is reserved for adults. The fitness center is open from 6 A.M. to 10 P.M.,

GAME ON!

Heads up, sports fans. There is a dedicated sports pub on each of the Disney cruise ships. The laid-back location is called Diversions. It's a sprawling, TV-filled room with a multitude of live events being broadcast at any time. There's often a mini-buffet available (think wings or hot dogs) and plenty of suds to wash down the snacks. (Snacks are free, but all beverages are extra.) If there's a particular game you're interested in, ask about it at the door. This spot is ideal for watching football, with up to six games shown at a time. Baseball is also a popular draw, as is the NBA. The occasional NHL game is shown, too. We love it here!

while the spa is open from 8 A.M. to 8 P.M.

Sports Deck

Deck 10 is home to the popular Wide World of Sports deck. Though open to everyone, it's a huge kid and teen magnet. The basketball hoops are hopping throughout the day. Basketballs and other equipment are on-site. There is no charge involved. This deck is also popular with casual strollers, though serious jogging is relegated to Deck 4 (where one lap is about a third of a mile).

Swimming

There are three guest swimming pools onboard, all located on Deck 9: Mickey's Pool (for kids) is located toward the back, or aft. Goofy's Family Pool is midship. And the Quiet Cove Adult Pool is on Deck 9, forward. Though the names are self-explanatory, we'll state the obvious: Mickey's pool is for the young'uns and their friends. The Quiet Cove pool is

earmarked strictly for splashers ages 18 and up. Don't let the name fool you; this pool may be for grown-ups, but it isn't always the picture of serenity. Organized games engage giddy adults from time to time. Finally, Goofy's pool is for everyone, but kids under 10 must be accompanied by an adult, and all swimmers must be potty-trained. Goofy's pool and Quiet Cove have two whirlpools each. Mickey's pool, which, incidentally, is in the shape of the Big Cheese's head, has a special element on the

Magic: the right, or starboard, ear is reserved for non-potty-trained guests. Kids should wear swim diapers. Diaper-wearing guests on the *Wonder* have their own special splash zone next to Mickey's Pool. (Swim diapers are a must.)

Vista Spa & Salon

Pampering, Disney style, can be enjoyed at this 10,700-square-foot ocean-view spa and salon, where fitness-minded folk can work with a qualified trainer and get instruction in aerobics, or work out in the fitness center. As for the pampering, well, that can come by way of any number of treatments.

Book appointments ahead of time by visiting *www.disneycruise.com*, or go directly to the spa when you first board the ship. Reservations aren't taken until 1 P.M., but the line forms fast. The Vista Spa and Salon is open to guests ages 18 and older.

It is open from 8 A.M. to 8 P.M. every day, *except* on days when the ship is docked at Port Canaveral. There is a fee for each treatment. Prices are posted in the spa. If you fail to show up for a reserved treatment, your stateroom will be charged. Note that Cabana Massages (offered on Castaway Cay) and the vista spa villas (luxurious and private indoor–outdoor treatment villas [available for one or two] at Vista Spa) are booked here

as well. Here's a sampling of treatments:

WELL BEING MASSAGE

This 50-minute treatment indulges the whole body and was created from cultural touches from around the world. Cost is about $109 per person, $242 per couple.

ELEMIS AROMA SPA OCEAN WRAP WITH HALF–BODY MASSAGE

The rather ambitious goal of this treatment is to help restore balance and harmony. Stress is eased away with a combination of aroma-therapy, a seaweed mask, and a blend of essential oils that is applied to your body before you are cocooned in a

HOT TIP

If you fail to get an appointment for a treatment at the spa, ask to be put on the waiting list—and be prepared to drop everything and run to the spa on a moment's notice.

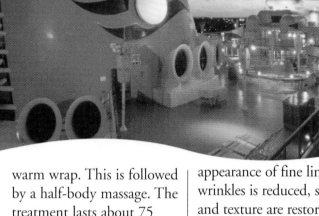

warm wrap. This is followed by a half-body massage. The treatment lasts about 75 minutes. Cost is $176.

HAIRDRESSING AND NAIL SERVICES

The salon offers hair styling, plus manicures and pedicures (including a milk-nourishing ritual for the hands and a peppermint ritual for the feet).

LA THERAPIE HYDRALIFT FACIAL

A "youth-enhancing" facial that promises fast and dramatic results. The appearance of fine lines and wrinkles is reduced, skin tone and texture are restored, and the complexion becomes smoother. The 50-minute treatment costs $109.

TROPICAL RAIN FOREST

Experience the benefits of steam, heat, and water therapy combined with the power of aromatherapy to relax the mind and body. Pair it with a treatment and a visit costs just $8. A one-day pass is $15. Unlimited cruise passes are available, too (prices vary).

PORTS OF CALL

To many travelers, the mere experience of being onboard a ship is reward enough; to others, the destinations are the reason to sail. To us, it is a little bit of each—so be it faraway places with strange-sounding names or luxurious beach resorts where you can sink your toes into the sand, these ports of call offer something for everyone.

We have made every effort to take all of the tours and excursion experiences described in this chapter; for those that we missed, we interviewed folks who did take them. That said, be aware that *none* of the shore excursions are run by Disney Cruise Line—not even those on Castaway Cay. While Disney strives to oversee the manner in which they are operated, levels of excellence vary from port to port and even from tour to tour. On the pages that follow, you'll find an overview of each port and brief-but-useful descriptions of any tours and adventures that are offered, followed by our personal experiences—both good and bad. Remember, you have the freedom to wander about and experience all ports of call at your leisure. This chapter is just meant to provide guidance should you be interested in signing up for "organized" fun.

Be aware that the tours described here may change without notice; we hope the general descriptions and personal views will aid you in your selection.

Enjoy.

COZUMEL

Welcome to the biggest island in Mexico! The 28-mile-long island, which gets its name from the Mayan phrase *cuzam huzil*, meaning "land of the swallows," is in the Caribbean, just 12 miles off the mainland. Home to the Palancar Reef (the second-largest diving reef in the world), it's no wonder that Cozumel is a magnet for underwater explorers and snorkelers.

Legend and lore abound here. Centuries ago, in about 300 A.D., the island was a shrine to Ixchel, the goddess of the moon and fertility. (It is said that, when angered, she vents her wrath through violent hurricanes and torrential rains. So don't make her angry. . . .)

The area is still rich in ancient sites. Here you will discover the history of a centuries-old culture in its ruins and churches, echoes of the past just waiting for modern-day explorers.

Cozumel is a scuba diver's paradise (it was a favorite destination of the late undersea explorer Jacques Cousteau). Its splendid coral reefs and tropical fish make it irresistible to divers, and fishing aficionados won't be disappointed either: The island's 600-feet-deep waters are populated by marlin, grouper, mackerel, and sailfish—in fact, several world sailfish records have been set here. Actually, it's a place for everyone—even golfers can satisfy an urge here. Intrigued? Read on.

SNORKELING ALERT

Snorkeling excursions are offered at most of the ports frequented by Disney Cruise Line. Olympic swimming skills aren't necessary, as all snorkelers are required to wear a life vest, but all guests should be comfortable in the water. Some tips:

- Before jumping in, ask the guide how much time you have and what signal to look for when it's time to return to the boat.
- The mask strap should rest above the ears (or it'll slip down the face).
- Keep hair out of the mask.
- If you can't see anything without your glasses, consider getting a prescription swimmer's mask before you leave home.
- If the mask fogs up, take it off and spit inside it. Rub the saliva around and replace the mask.
- If water gets in the breathing tube, blow hard through the tube or remove the mouthpiece and empty.
- Bring an underwater camera—and wrap the strap around your wrist.
- Listen to your guide: he or she will alert you to any potential danger.
- There is a first-aid kit on the boat for minor cuts and scrapes.
- Bring a towel from the Disney ship. You'll need it. (Don't forget to bring it back!)

Cozumel's Golf Excursion
(6 hours; Ages 10 and up)

No need to forgo the island atmosphere while you enjoy your favorite sport: The Cozumel Country Club's lush grounds offer swaying palms and ocean breezes along with 18 holes of golf. Balls, cart fees, greens fees, and souvenir balls are included in the cost of the excursion; club and shoe rentals and lunch are available at an extra charge.

 Our not-so-scientific survey about this excursion yielded nothing but praise for the experience.

⚓ Adults: $145 (ages 10 and above)
Departure Time: 9:45 A.M.

Certified Scuba Tour
(4.5 hours; Ages 12 and up)

If you're a certified diver (you must present your certified dive card and have participated in a dive within the last two years), this is a not-to-be-missed experience.

After being briefed about the dive plan and safety tips, you'll dive Palancar Reef to depths of 70 to 80 feet; along these coral atolls you'll see spotted moray, snake eels, trumpet fish, grunt, and angel fish, and between the coral columns are white-sand passageways and intricate caverns. Once you resurface you can enjoy a light snack as you head for the next (50 to 60 feet) dive site. All scuba equipment is provided.

 This was a first-rate experience; our guide was knowledgeable, and the view below was undeniably awesome.

⚓ Adults: $94 (ages 12 and above)
   Departure Time: 11:35 A.M.

Dolphin Discovery Cozumel
(3–3.5 hours; Ages 3 and up)

Here's an opportunity for the whole family to get up close and personal with one of the sea's friendliest creatures. Dolphins are the star attractions on this tour to Chankanaab National Park, where you stand in waist-high water and watch as one of Mother Nature's cleverest marine mammals frolics at your feet. Afterward, enjoy the rest of the park—there's a beach for snorkeling and a replica of Mayan ruins.

 This tour was a tad tame for those with an adventuresome spirit—yet young kids loved it, so we recommend this for families traveling with children. Others might find it a bit understimulating, though the Mayan ruins replica was interesting.

⚓ Adults: $110 (ages 10 and above)
   Children: $96 (ages 3–9)
   Departure Times: 10:45 A.M.;
   11:45 A.M.; 12:45 P.M.

Discover Snorkel
(3 hours; Ages 5 and up)

Never snorkeled before? Here's a chance to get your feet wet. The experience begins with a crash-course in the basics of snorkeling. Seasoned snorkelers should pay attention, too—it never hurts to brush up a bit. After the session of Snorkeling 101, you're free to explore reefs and mingle with marine life in the tranquil waters of Cozumel.

Mother Nature really knows how to put on a show. The non-air-conditioned cab ride is a drag, though. Bring a fan!

⚓ Adults: $32 (ages 10 and above)
   Children: $23 (ages 5–9)
   Departure Time: 10:45 A.M

Mayan Frontier Horseback Riding Tour
(4 hours; Ages 12 and up)

You'll really think you've traveled back in time (way back to about 2000 B.C.) when you hop on a horse and see replicas of ruins along the Mayan frontier, a tropical savanna with echoes of another era. Visit a working ranch stocked with cattle, ponies, and other requisite ranch critters. When you're done, soft drinks and beer await you before you return to the ship—and the 21st century.

Equestrians were pleased with this one. It was well run and good for riders of all ages. It is most enjoyable when the temperature is on the less-than-steamy side.

⚓ Adults: $85 (ages 12 and above)
   Departure Time: 10:15 A.M.
   Maximum weight: 240 lbs.

Tulum Ruins
(7.5 hours; Ages 5 and up)

Imagine leaving your cruise
ship and boarding a bus to
the past. That's what you'll
do on this archaeological
tour. The sacred Mayan
city of Tulum is the
destination, a knowledgeable
guide is your invaluable
companion, and the remnants of a
fascinating civilization are yours to explore. There's time
(about two hours) to enjoy the nearby beach, and soft
drinks and sandwiches are included in the price of the tour.
A few notes: There is an additional charge to use *your own*
video camera. Since the terrain is not stroller friendly (read:
not allowed) and requires a lot of walking, this tour is not
recommended for children under eight.

*While fascinating, this is a very long day. Our guide was
informative, but our hardy crew agreed that this is best
left to the archaeological-minded traveler. Kids may get
restless—there's a lot of travel time.*

⚓ Adults: $97 (ages 10 and above)
  Children: $72 (ages 5–9)
  Departure Time: 9:15 A.M.

Jeep Exploration
(4.5 hours; Ages 10 and up)

Buckle up and prepare for a memorable—if very bumpy— journey of discovery on this guided Jeep tour into ancient Mexico. After the tour, there's time to hit the beach (a Mexican-style lunch is provided). Jeeps accommodate groups of four. The driving is shared among guests, so be sure to bring your driver's license—and be aware that it's a stick shift here (as in, no automatic transmission).

Unless you are an experienced (and we do mean experienced) driver, skip this one. To describe the terrain as bumpy is an understatement. The beach is nice, but not necessarily worth the grueling ride.

⚓ Adults: $85 (ages 10 and above)
Departure Time: 9:45 A.M.

Dolphin Discovery Observer
(3–3.5 hours; Ages 3 and up)

Consider this an opportunity to get up close, but not too personal, with our dolphin friends. As opposed to Dolphin Discovery Cozumel (page 105), guests stay dry and watch dolphins from a distance. A member of the group may get a close encounter of the dolphin kind, but there's no guarantee. Afterward, feel free to enjoy the beach at Chankanaab National Park. There are opportunities to buy food and souvenirs, too. Guests using wheelchairs must be sure the chair is collapsible, to fit into the taxi (which is not air-conditioned, by the way.)

What We Heard

It's a more cost-efficient way to spy on these delightful ocean dwellers—but not quite as rewarding as the Dolphin Discovery Cozumel excursion (page 105). Still, the kiddies really dig those dolphins.

⚓ Adults: $40 (ages 10 and above)
   Children: $40 (ages 3–9)
   Departure Times: 9:45 A.M.; 12 P.M.

Fury Catamaran Sail, Snorkel, and Beach Party
(4.5–5 hours; Ages 5 and up)

Enjoy the best of all possible worlds on this outing. Your magic carpet is a luxurious 65-foot catamaran replete with sundeck and shady areas. The day includes a snorkeling adventure (all equipment provided) and a beach party complete with kayaks and volleyball. If that's not enough, complimentary soft drinks, margaritas, and beer are yours for the asking (as long as you're at least 21 years old).

Adventurous types, especially teens, love this one. After the snorkeling, the party really gets under way—and the grown-ups find the margaritas marvelous.

⚓ Adults: $49 (ages 10 and above)
Children: $28 (ages 5–9)
Departure Time: 12:45 P.M.

Eco-Park & Snorkel
(4.25 hours; Ages 3 and up [must be at least age 5 to snorkel])

Feeling rugged? Grab your hiking shoes and climb aboard an open-air, all-terrain vehicle. About 35 minutes later, you'll tour Punta Sur Ecological Park. Among the highlights: a crocodile-filled lagoon, an ancient Mayan structure, and the Punta Sur Lighthouse and Nautical Museum. Chase that with some sun worshipping on the beach or a beginner's snorkel adventure.

The trip is taxing, but the park is pretty. The snorkel "adventure" is pretty tame. Good for beginners.

⚓ Adults: $49 (ages 10 and above)
Children: $34 (ages 3–9)
Departure Time: 12:45 P.M.

Xcaret Eco Archaeological Park
(7–7.5 hours; All ages)

There's so much to see here that Disney has decided to leave you on your own to explore. Snorkel (equipment is *not* included, but is available to rent), soak up some culture at the museum, visit the aquarium and bird sanctuary, stop at the stables, delight in the blooms at the botanical gardens, explore the ancient ruins. It's all here. Did we mention the beautiful beaches? Or the lunch and transportation to the park? Enough said.

Many folks said that this is a good way to take in a little bit of everything in a lot of hours. Young children got cranky by the end of the day, but overall the reports were positive.

⚓ Adults: $99
(ages 10 and above)
Children: $77 (ages 9 and under)
Departure Time: 9:15 A.M.

Mexican Cuisine Workshop & Tasting
(5–5.5 hours; Ages 14 and up)

You're in Mexico. What better place to get a crash course in Mexican cuisine? After a 25-minute ride to Playa Mia Grand Beach Park, an expert chef shares "scrumptious secrets" and guides guests as they prepare a full-course feast. Folks who've already celebrated their 21st birthday may enjoy the open bar while they cook. Following the 2-hour food fiesta, there's time to swim or relax on the beach before heading back to the ship. Note that all participants must be able to stand for at least one hour.

It's a nice alternative to the more active, water-oriented excursions. Yet standing for more than an hour isn't for everyone.

⚓ Adults: $69 (ages 14 and above)
Departure Time: 10:45 A.M.

Dune Buggy & Beach Snorkel Combo
(4–4.5 hours; Ages 10 and up)

Guests board a customized dune buggy—a four-seater convertible—for a quick trip to a 60-minute snorkel experience. After bonding with fishes, it's back to the buggy for a scenic (if lengthy) drive to the beach. Expect to enjoy about an hour at the ocean's edge. A Mexican snack buffet is provided. There are shopping opportunities, so you may want to bring some cash.

Dune buggies rock! And you might even get to drive—provided that you're 18 years old and have a valid driver's license. Of course, we're always up for snorkeling and sun worshipping, but could do without the long commute.

⚓ Adults: $90 (ages 10 and above)
  Departure Time: 9:45 A.M.

Power Snorkel Treasure Hunt
(3 hours; Ages 12 and up)

Snorkeling with a twist. Sure, there'll be plenty of sea creatures to ogle—but you're here to find treasure of a different kind: gold coins. After a 20-minute taxi ride, guests get snorkel gear, a Sea Doo Scooter (personal propellant device), and a lesson. After that, it's all about hunting for booty. A snack is served.

Your competitive nature may make an appearance while diving for doubloons, but it's all in good fun. The Sea Doo Scooter is a nice touch.

⚓ Adults: $59 (ages 12 and above)
  Departure Time: 1:50 P.M.

Cozumel Beach Break
(4.5–5 hours; All ages)

Playa Sol is a place for splashing in the pool, lying on the sand, waterskiing, and prancing at the playground. It's all here and all yours for a four-hour respite from—well, from all your other cruising respites. Included in the fee is admission to the pool and use of beach facilities, water toys, and other games. There is an open bar serving mixed drinks, beer, soda, and juice, and a buffet lunch is provided. The beach is accessible via taxi from the pier. There's an additional charge for motorized water sports.

 A nice outing. We always enjoy a day at the beach.

⚓ Adults: $59 (ages 10 and above)
    Children: $46 (ages 3–9)
    Under age 3: free
    Departure Time: 10:10 A.M.

Speed Boat Beach Escape
(5 hours; Ages 10 and up)

Barracuda Beach is the place where you can take the wheel of a two-person speed boat (maximum speed: 20 mph) and take an hour-long tour of the turquoise waters of the Caribbean. Afterward, consider relaxing or playing some volleyball back on Barracuda Beach. A light buffet and beverages are provided. Guests must be at least 18 and be a bearer of a valid driver's license in order to drive. The beach is about a 20-minute taxi ride from the ship.

 Other than the 5-hour time commitment, the only real drawback is that you have two people per boat. It's more fun for the driver.

⚓ Adults: $85 (ages 10 and above)
    Departure Time: 8:30 A.M.

Caverns Exploration and Beach Tour

(7–7.5 hours; Ages 6 and up)

A guided tour of these natural caverns near Playa del Carmen will give you a close encounter with stalactites and stalagmites. After the casual spelunking, you get to relax at the beach—in your own beach chair—and enjoy a Mexican-style lunch. Note that due to the rough terrain, strollers are not allowed on this tour.

Curious amateur spelunkers found this interesting; beach lovers preferred that portion of the day. But some said it wasn't worth the hefty price.

⚓ Adults: $88 (ages 10 and above)
Children: $63 (ages 6–9)
Departure Time: 9:15 A.M.

Atlantis Submarine Expedition

(2–2.5 hours; Ages 4 and up)

Get a fish's-eye view of the colorful world under the sea, thanks to the U.S. Coast Guard certified submarine *Atlantis*. As the sub dives 110 feet into the deep, guests see tropical fish and towering coral formations while a narrator makes the wonder of it all even more wonderful. Once the boat surfaces, passengers will have yet another treat—free rum and fruit punch.

We met some parents who took their kids (ages 6 and 10) down under. The fact that fresh air was circulating at all times made it a kid-friendly experience. And although we enjoyed the tour, we recommend that claustrophobes avoid this one.

⚓ Adults: $89 (ages 10 and above)
Children: $57 (ages 4–9; must be at least 36 inches tall)
Departure Times: 11:45 A.M.; 12:45 P.M.

Cozumel Ruins and Beach Tour
(4–4.5 hours; Ages 5 and up)

Culture and leisure go hand in hand on this guided tour where you explore the ancient history of Cozumel at the San Gervasio Ruins, a Mayan religious center, and then chill out at Playa Sol Adventure Park for an hour and a half of swimming and water sports (there is an additional charge for equipment). The terrain is rough here, so strollers are not allowed.

The terrain wasn't only too rough for baby strollers—it was tough for adult "strollers" too.

⚓ Adults: $49 (ages 10 and above)
  Children: $33 (ages 5–9)
  Departure Time: 12 P.M.

OTHER PORTS OF CALL

On special sailings, usually during the Christmas holidays, the *Disney Magic* adds a couple of destinations to its cruises. The trade-off (there always is one) is that you may have to sacrifice two of those leisurely sea days. But if these ports appeal to you, remember, this extra-special sailing only happens once or twice a year. Check with your travel agent for dates. Know that special cruises are very popular and tend to sell out far in advance. For information on upcoming special sailings, pay a visit to *www.disneycruise.com* or call 800-910-3659.

Clear Kayak and Beach Snorkel
(3.5 hours; Ages 10 and up)

A visit to one of Cozumel's newest beach clubs, the exclusive Uvas Beach, includes a 45-minute guided kayaking experience, plus 40 minutes of spying on undersea critters with provided snorkel equipment, and a chance to splash in the ocean, play in the sand, or snooze on the beach.

 The kayak experience is not for wimps! We like having the choice to snorkel or not to snorkel—since the allotted beach time (45 minutes) simply isn't enough for us.

⚓ Adults: $61 (ages 10 and above)
Departure Time: 1:15 P.M.

Jungle Bike Adventure
(4.5 hours; Ages 10 and up)

For serious bikers only, this 6-mile journey takes you to several partially excavated Mayan ruins while learning the history of the ancient civilization (courtesy of your well-informed guide). A bottle of water and small snack are provided. Guests are encouraged to bring backpacks with additional supplies. Participants need to be at least 48 inches tall and weigh less than 250 pounds. Closed-toed shoes are a must. The excursion involves a one-hour, round-trip bus ride.

 We're not big fans of sweaty bike marathons, but that's just us. For some, this might be the perfect way to explore Cozumel.

⚓ Adults: $52 (ages 10 and above)
Departure Time: 9 A.M.

Ocean View Explorer Tour
(2 hours; All ages)

Look below! This glass-bottom boat lets you see underwater without getting your feet wet. Fish, other fascinating marine life, and colossal coral formations of Paradiso reef appear before your eyes. There's not a bad seat in the house—er, boat.

If you absolutely, positively don't want to go into the water, this is a nice opportunity to spy on creatures of the deep.

⚓ Adults: $42 (ages 10 and above)
Children: $31 (ages 9 and under)
Departure Time: 10:45 A.M.

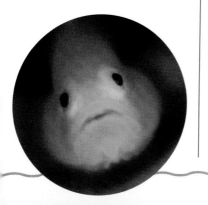

Jungle Hike Expedition
(4 hours; Ages 10 and up)

After a 30-minute bus trip, guests are deposited at a hiking station. They're given backpacks stuffed with binoculars, a compass, an explorer booklet, a bottle of water, and a snack. (Everything but the water and snack must be returned.) A guide takes you on a tour of approximately two miles of lush tropical terrain, including a peek at some Mayan ruins. Shoes must have closed toes. Take extra rations.

Less physically taxing than the Jungle Bike Adventure (page 116), this experience is certainly memorable. (Though we'd skip it if the temperature is soaring.)

⚓ Adults: $58 (ages 10 and above)
Departure Time: 9 A.M.

Dolphin Trainer for a Day
(5.5 hours; Ages 10 and up)

After a brief taxi ride, guests arrive at Dolphinaris, one of the few places in the world to offer guests the chance to enjoy up-close encounters with enchanting marine mammals. The day begins with a 50-minute primer on our flippered friends, followed by snack time— for the dolphins *and* the humans. After a 45-minute snorkel session, it's "face-to-flipper" time. You'll no doubt marvel as dolphins complete tasks at your command. For some, it's all about the belly ride. (Hang on!) Lunch is included.

If you are a physically fit dolphin fan, it doesn't get better than this! It's a long day, but quite rewarding.

⚓ Adults: $285 (ages 10 and above)

Dolphin Kids at Dolphinaris
(3 hours; Ages 4 to 9)

After a kid-friendly intro to dolphins (including a discussion of anatomy, physiology, and history), guests experience a close encounter with Pacific bottlenose dolphins. Under the supervision of a trainer, children enjoy 40 minutes of interacting with the friendly mammals. The experience is capped with a little dolphin showboating (kisses, hugs, and jumps). Kids must be accompanied by a parent or guardian on the dolphin Observer at Dolphinaris excursion (see page 121).

Thrilling for most youngsters, though some little ones might be a bit spooked by the up-close-encounter with the enormous creatures. They may also get squirmy during the lesson. Older kids dig it.

⚓ Children: $105 (ages 4 to 9)

Dolphin Swim at Dolphinaris
(3 hours; Ages 5 and up)

Following a brief dolphin lesson, guests make their way to a submerged (waist deep) platform and enjoy an in-water exchange with real live bottlenose dolphins. You'll learn how dolphins respond to hand signals, get some hands-on time with the crafty mammals, and even share a kiss with one of your newfound friends (or a handshake for the modest). The bonding continues in the deeper coves area, where everyone is treated to a belly-ride, courtesy of our fine flippered-friends.

For us, 40 minutes of quality time with these magical creatures is priceless. Though the actual price is a bit hefty! Still, it's a gem of an experience.

⚓ Adults: $160 (ages 10 and above)

  Children: $145 (ages 5 to 9)

Luxury Yacht Charter
(4–4.5 hours; All ages)

What's better than a private Caribbean cruise for 10? One with a 2-hour beach break, plus lunch (lobster and steamed veggies) and cocktails. Each 46-foot motor-powered yacht comes with a captain and first-mate, as well as two cabins with surround-sound stereo systems, two bathrooms (with showers), sun pads, and floating mats. Snorkel equipment is provided at the beach. Wheelchairs are not permitted.

Luxury is the operative word here. There is definitely something special about commandeering a fancy yacht for a day. And the beach is quite lovely.

⚓ Adults: Price based on boat

  Children: Price based on boat

Discover Mexico & Chankanaab
(5 hours; Ages 5 and up)

Celebrating Mexico from the pre-Hispanic age to modern times, Discover Mexico is a cultural park brimming with exhibits for the whole family. Expect to spend about 75 minutes exploring this facility before moving on (via taxi) to Chankanaab Park. This spot boasts more than 350 species of plants and is awash with tropical fish and colorful underwater vistas. Break out the snorkel equipment pronto! If that's not your thing, feel free to relax on the beach or set out on a nature walk. Lunch is included.

What We Think

Tackling two compelling parks in 5 hours is a tad ambitious, but still worthwhile.

⚓ Adults: $59 (ages 10 and above)
Children: $39 (ages 5 to 9)

Four Elements—A Mayan Adventure
(7 hours; Ages 10 and up)

Are you physically fit and itching for an adventure? This 7-hour experience will whisk you to Chikin-Ha—a protected natural sanctuary—and immerse you in Mayan culture. Activities highlight primal elements of earth, water, wind, and fire. Expect to bike through farmlands, snorkel in natural limestone sinkholes, and even fly above the jungle (on a zip-line). This excursion is best enjoyed by active folks. It's not for anyone with any physical limitations whatsoever.

We admit it: We are just too doughy to get the most out of this experience. Daredevils and gym rats, on the other hand, more than get their money's worth.

⚓ Adults: $99 (ages 10 and above)

Dolphin Observer at Dolphinaris
(3 hours; Ages 3 and up)

This excursion lets water-wary guests observe friends or family as they "swim" with the dolphins. "Observers" are treated to the same overview of dolphins, including their amazing history and under-water communication system. After that, they relax and watch loved ones interact with dolphins in a pool and ocean cove setting. Talk about a photo op! (This excursion must be booked in conjunction with Dolphin Swim at Dolphinaris, Dolphin Trainer for a Day, or Dolphin Kids at Dolphinaris.)

We prefer dolphin encounters from anear (not afar!), but this is an ideal way to bond with loved ones as they bond with the sea mammals.

⚓ Adults: $25 (ages 10 and above)
   Children: $25 (ages 3 to 9)

GRAND CAYMAN

In 1503, when Christopher Columbus came upon these islands (there are actually three Caymans: Grand Cayman, at 76 square miles, is the largest; Little Cayman; and Cayman Brac), he named them *Las Tortugas*, a nod to the then large turtle population here. The present name is closer to *caymanas*, the Spanish-Carib word for alligators, although the nearest relatives you'll find here are iguanas. What you *will* find are big bucks (the paper kind, that is). George Town, the capital city of Grand Cayman island, is one of the world's largest financial centers, home to more than 500 banks.

Of much greater interest to leisure travelers is that the sparkling waters off its Caribbean shores make Grand Cayman a snorkeler's and diver's dream. In fact, it's one of the top five dive destinations in the world. Waters teem with coral and fish, and even non-swimmers can get a view of these underwater wonders— including the Cayman Wall and its resident population of stingrays—from a glass-bottom boat or mini-sub.

Shoppers should head for Fort Street and Cardinal Avenue. *Note:* Although you may be tempted, steer clear of all items made from turtle and black coral. Both are endangered species. (In fact, items made from sea turtle cannot be brought back to the United States.) Opt instead for some of the interesting jewelry fashioned from shipwreck artifacts— some old gold pieces, perhaps? And if hunger strikes, have lunch in town. Our favorite island treat is conch (pronounced *konk*)—as fritters or in chowder. Trust us, it's delicious.

If you are fans of all things Disney but think that a Disney cruise might be too, um, cutesy for your taste, you might be surprised. Adult tastes and sensibilities are factored into the overall equation for the Disney ships. Sure, kids abound (they even have their own deck), but you have your own pool, restaurant, and spa. Come sundown, the over-18 set can mosey over to Route 66 (*Wonder*) or Beat Street (*Magic*)—and enjoy a festive cluster of entertainment venues earmarked exclusively for the grown-up set.

At many ports of call there are tours—scuba, snorkeling, golfing, and the like—where the under-18 crowd can't crowd you. In fact, on Castaway Cay, Disney's own private island, you can bask in the sun or read a novel in the shade of a magnolia tree on a beach designated especially for grown-ups. You can even have a massage in a private cabana overlooking the ocean.

After all, this is your vacation, and it's understandable that you'd expect some measure of privacy and more than a modicum of peace and quiet, and grown-up fun. And, of course, bingo.

Sea Trek Grand Cayman
(1.5 hours; Ages 10 and up)

It's more than snorkeling, yet it's not quite scuba diving. Here guests get to explore the crystal-blue waters in a "helmet-diving" experience. The specially designed oxygen helmet lets you immerse yourself below sea level for a fun-filled 30-minute guided tour. Though folks need not have a diving or snorkeling background, it helps to be in strong physical shape.

We are flat-out fascinated by this helmet contraption. It allows all the joys of snorkeling without swallowing any of the sea! Can be a tad claustrophobic, though.

⚓ Adults: $85 (ages 10 and above)
   Departure Times: 8:30 A.M.;
   10:30 A.M.; 11:30 A.M.

2-Tank Dive Tour
(4.5 hours; Ages 12 and up)

There's deep, and then there's not so deep; sink to both levels on this two-tank dive, first to 80 feet at the Cayman Wall to see a veritable rainbow of tropical fish and coral, then to a shallower dive (only 50 feet) at a reef or shipwreck. All equipment (except wet suits, which have an additional fee) is provided.

This is a diver's delight. Everything we signed up for was there; the colors were amazing, and the shipwreck was a hoot.

⚓ Adults: $135 (ages 12 and above; not recommended for younger children)
Departure Time: 7:45 A.M.

Nautilus Undersea Tour and Reef Snorkel

(3 hours; Ages 5 and up)

Here's an opportunity to see the sea from both above and below. Onboard the *Nautilus*, the world's largest semi-submarine, you'll sail over some spectacular shipwrecks and out to Cheeseburger Reef. As for the "below" part of the adventure: Don your goggles and snorkel with the rainbow of tropical fish that call this home. Snorkel gear is included.

"A nice day" was mostly what we heard about this tour. Folks expected more when they heard the word "Nautilus" (like deep dives and so on), but they generally enjoyed the time and felt it was worth the money.

⚓ Adults: $49 (ages 10 and above)
Children: $43 (ages 5–9)
Departure Time: 7:30 A.M.

Pirate Encounter

(2.5 hours; Ages 3 and up)

This excursion could be called "We Wanna Walk the Plank!" A short tender boat trip takes guests to one of the world's last wooden brigs, *Valhalla*. Friendly pirates are there to welcome you aboard, sail the ship past Seven Mile Beach, and make you walk to the plank (don't worry, you don't have to jump, but you should—it's a lot of fun!). Figure on about 40 minutes of splashing around time.

Who knew how much fun it would be to jump off the side of a pirate ship—again and again and again?! It's not for guests with limited mobility, but young'uns love the pirate factor.

⚓ Adults: $35 (ages 10 and above)
Children: $25 (ages 3–9)
Departure Times: 9:30 A.M.; 12:30 P.M.

Stingray City Snorkel Tour
(3.5 hours; Ages 5 and up)

Stingrays are among the most fascinating—and usually docile—sea creatures you'll ever encounter. A catamaran ride to world-famous Stingray City is rewarded with countless rays residing in 3 to 6 feet of water on a natural sandbar. Be daring: You can snorkel amid the rays. All equipment is provided, and once you touch land, cold water and lemonade await.

This had the potential to be a spectacular experience, but the described "short" catamaran ride was a half hour long and the time spent with the stingrays was a mere 20 minutes. Still, an enjoyable trip.

⚓ Adults: $47 (ages 10 and above)
   Children: $36 (ages 5–9)
   Departure Times: 7:20 A.M.; 10 A.M.

HOT TIP

While ashore waiting for tours to gather, be sure to pick a shady spot where you can easily spot your group.

Boatswain's Adventure Marine Park
(4.5–5 hours; All ages)

Turtles, lizards, and sharks—oh, my! You'll see them all at Boatswain's Adventure Marine Park. The shoreside retreat is home to more than 11,000 turtles at the historic Cayman Turtle Farm. There's also a 1.3 million–gallon lagoon that's teeming with wildlife. You may take a stroll down the Nature Trail (if you want to see those lizards), shop on Cayman Street, and/or dive into Breaker's lagoon. Snorkel equipment is provided, food is not (though it is possible to buy some).

It's a bit pricey, but you get a lot for the money. A must for turtle fans.

⚓ Adults: $92 (ages 10 and above)
   Children: $52 (ages 3–9)
   Under age 3: free

Stingray City Reef Sail and Snorkel
(3.5 hours; Ages 5 and up)

No mere dip-your-face-in-the-
water-near-the-shore experience,
this seven-mile adventure aboard a
65-foot catamaran gives you an
opportunity to explore the deep, study
the coral formations, and watch fish cavort before your eyes.
All snorkeling equipment, water, and soft drinks are provided.

*Members of our group went on this tour and gave it high marks.
The snorkeling location for this one was quieter, and a
knowledgeable guide enriched the experience immensely. A good
time was had by all—even the fish.*

⚓ Adults: $58 (ages 10 and above)
   Children: $45 (ages 5–9)
   Departure Times: 8 A.M.; 12 P.M.

Seaworld Explorer Semi-Submarine
(1.5 hours; All ages)

Down periscope! It's time to submerge for a look at the treasures under the sea on this semi-submarine that takes you to two incredible shipwrecks, and allows you to get an underwater view of an unforgettable array of sea life. Best of all, you'll have a marine expert onboard to give you some history and answer all of your questions.

The shipwrecks were fun to look at, and the fish were fabulous. The guide made the history of the area come to life. A winner.

⚓ Adults: $43 (ages 10 and above)
Children: $31 (ages 9 and under)
Departure Time: 8:20 A.M.

129

Atlantis Submarine Expedition
(2.5 hours; Ages 4 and up)

Have you ever heard of barrel sponges? Neither had we until we took this underwater tour aboard the *Atlantis XI* sub and saw them through the portholes (they're among the world's largest sponges). We also saw star corals, stingrays, turtles, and other exotic fish.

We liked this one. Not only because it was like taking a course in Sponges 101, but the fish (we're suckers for stingrays) were the stars of the day.

⚓ Adults: $89 (ages 10 and above)
Children: $57 (ages 4–9; must be at least 36 inches tall)
Departure Times: 9:40 A.M.; 1:15 P.M.

Island Tour & Butterfly Farm
(3.5 hours; Ages 3 and up)

After a taking a peek at the Governor's house on scenic Seven Mile Beach, the 25-minute bus tour stops at the world's only green sea turtle farm. Next up: "Hell"—so named for its unusual coral formation. Then it's off to a more heavenly encounter with colorful, winged creatures in a tropical garden at Grand Cayman's Butterfly Farm. The journey is chased with a visit to the original Tortuga rum cake factory, where tastings are a-plenty.

The bus tour is brief but enjoyable, as were the turtles—but the Butterfly Farm is the star. And if rum cake's your thing, you're in luck!

⚓ Adults: $59 (ages 10 and above)
Children: $43 (ages 3–9)
Departure Times: 8 A.M.; 12 P.M.

Nautilus Undersea Tour
(2 hours; All ages)

If *under* water isn't your thing, then try this very impressive alternative. The *Nautilus* glides like a boat and gives you a glorious underwater view like a sub, but never completely submerges. What's more, you get to view the deep (without actually going there) in a spacious, air-conditioned underwater observatory. Best of all, the wonders of life below come alive as an expert marine narrator regales you with tales of the sea on this amazing tour of shipwrecks, sea life, and incredible coral reefs.

"Great for landlubbers, like us" is what we heard from folks who took this tour. The comfort level onboard was excellent.

⚓ Adults: $42 (ages 10 and above)
   Children: $31 (agse 9 and under)
   Departure Time: 9 A.M.

Rum Point Beach Adventure
(5.5 hours; All ages)

Life really is a beach on this day of doing absolutely nothing on a beach that affords you absolutely everything. Only a short bus and ferry ride away, Rum Point is *the* place to go for swimming, sunning, or relaxing. Tropical sound effects include casuarina trees rustling overhead. Sandwiches and beverages are included in this day of total indulgence. For more active folk, various water sports are available for an additional cost.

The beach bums in our group thought this was the ultimate. So if you fall into that category, take note.

⚓ Adults: $54 (ages 10 and above)
Children: $46 (ages 9 and under)
Departure Time: 8:20 A.M.

Rum Point Beach Adventure and Stingray City Snorkel
(5.5 hours; Ages 5 and up)

Look at the tour on page 128, add a glass-bottom boat ride to Stingray City where you can snorkel with the stingrays, and you know what we mean when we say, "Having it all."

What We Think

And the snorkeling was cool, too! (See page 128.)

⚓ Adults: $89 (ages 10 and above)
   Children: $79 (ages 5–9)
   Departure Time: 8:20 A.M.

WILL YOU MARRY ME—AGAIN?

Whether you're celebrating your first, fifteenth, or fiftieth, renewing your vows can be a life-affirming experience. Those couples who still feel like newlyweds long after the wedding day know that anniversaries can mark more than years. What better way to say "I love you still" than by having another wedding? Perhaps your first "I do's" were said in front of a justice of the peace; now you can don that white gown and do it up in grand style. Or, if you prefer to keep it low-key, a small corsage and boutonniere will do just fine. An officer of the *Disney Magic* or *Disney Wonder* can perform the ceremony. Ask the kids along this time (chances are they weren't present for the first go-round) or make it a very private affair with just the two of you, as it was at the beginning. We can't tell you how many couples have decided to renew their vows on the Disney ships; suffice it to say that there's a lot of hand-holding, slow dancing, and stolen kisses to be seen on deck. For more information, call (407) 828-3400.

Shipwreck and Reef Snorkeling
(2–2.5 hours; Ages 5 and up)

First stop is the *Callie*, one of the Caymans' most famous wrecks. Onboard, experienced dive masters provide a history of the ship plus give those who need it some instruction in snorkeling. The next stop affords you the opportunity to view some spectacular coral reef formations and tropical fish; you may even spot a turtle. Snorkeling equipment, ice water, and lemonade are provided.

This tour proved a major favorite among the people we spoke to. They loved the snorkeling and the shipwreck—and one of them saw a huge turtle. Excellent, dude.

⚓ Adults: $37 (ages 10 and above)
   Children: $31 (ages 5–9)
   Departure Times: 8 A.M.; 10:30 A.M.

Grand Cayman Island Tour
(2 hours; All ages)

Although most folks head for the island's shores, the curious explorer should know that Grand Cayman is more than a beach—much more. And you'll discover this on an air-conditioned bus that meanders through the quaint streets of George Town and past the storybook-perfect gingerbread houses to the odd rock formations of an eerie island wonder called "Hell." Then it's on to the world's only turtle breeding operation of its kind, Cayman Turtle Farm.

We were a little disappointed in this one. The turtles were interesting, but not worth the outing.

⚓ Adults: $29 (ages 10 and above)
Children: $24 (ages 3–9)
Under age 3: free
Departure Times: 8:15 A.M.;
11:45 A.M.

Island Tour and Snorkeling with Stingrays
(4 hours; Ages 5 and up)

A veritable smorgasbord of adventures, this tour lets you do it all in a scant 4 hours. First, it's a stop at world-famous Seven Mile Beach, then a chance to experience classic island architecture with a trip to Old Homestead, and for nature lovers, a visit to the Cayman Turtle Farm. Naturalists will appreciate the island's prehistoric rock formation, a place the locals call "Hell." And last, but certainly not least, head to Stingray Sandbar to get up close and personal with sea life. Snorkeling equipment is provided.

The turtle farm was just okay, but the snorkeling made up for it. You gotta love those stingrays.

⚓ Adults: $63 (ages 10 and above)
Children: $52 (ages 5–9)
Departure Times: 9:45 A.M.;
11:45 A.M.

Thriller Sea and Sand Adventure
(3 hours; Ages 5 and up)

The Grand Cayman *Thriller* boat speeds along the shoreline for about 45 minutes before depositing guests on the white sands of Sea Grape Beach. Complimentary soda or bottled water is included (as are lounge chairs), whereas items from the grill cost extra.

The boat ride is fun, but we wish there was more time to play on the beach. (We always do!)

⚓ Adults: $69 (ages 10 and above)
Children: $49 (ages 5–9)
Departure Time: 9:20 A.M.

Seven Mile Beach Break
(4.5 hours; All ages)

A short bus ride is all it takes to get to Grand Cayman's newest beach destination: Sea Grape Beach. So grab a lounge chair, a complimentary soft drink, sit back, relax, and enjoy. Take some cash along, as there's an opportunity to buy grilled snacks and other beverages.

A beach day we can get excited about! The transportation-beach time ratio is just right, as is the area of beach that's reserved for Disney Cruise Line guests. And the price is right.

⚓ Adults: $36 (ages 10 and above)
Children: $26 (ages 5–9); Under age 3: free
Departure Times: 7:50 A.M.; 10:30 A.M.

Aquaboat and Snorkel Adventure
(3 hours; Ages 10 and up)

Head for the high seas aboard a two-person inflatable motorboat, which you'll then pilot along Grand Cayman's scenic shores (there are instructors to show you how to maneuver the craft; "captains" must be 13 or older to drive and be accompanied by a parent or guardian 18 or older). Make a stop and explore the uninhabited Sandy Cay, just off the Cayman coast; then enjoy some R & R at Smith's Cove, a picturesque bay and secluded beach where you can swim, snorkel, or just chill on the beach. Well rested, you take the wheel again and head for the *Callie*, a submerged shipwreck, before returning to the dock and heading to Rackams Bar for a complimentary fruit or rum punch.

What We Heard

This was a banner day for most boat lovers who took the tour. Some parents didn't feel comfortable allowing their kids to pilot the boat, however. The scenery is amazing, and Smith's Cove was the icing on the cake. The shipwreck, we heard, was excellent and the rum punch scored high.

⚓ Adults: $84 (per guest, with a maximum of two in a boat; ages 10 and above—not recommended for young children)
Departure Time: 12 noon
Maximum weight: 400 lbs. per boat

DISNEY'S NOD TO NATURE

In its ongoing attempt to maintain the integrity of the land and sea, the ecology-minded folks at Disney Cruise Line have taken the following steps:

⚓ Every sailing, the Disney ships recycle tons of aluminum, clean cardboard, and plastic.

⚓ Between the two cruise ships, enough plastic water bottles are collected each year to span 49 miles. That's about the distance from Port Canaveral to Orlando! In all, Disney Cruise Line recycles more than a half million bottles a year.

⚓ Guests at Castaway Cay are urged to follow the "take only memories, leave only footprints" policy prohibiting the removal of shells—which are often homes for marine creatures—from the island.

⚓ Mini-reefs are being cultivated in Castaway Cay's snorkeling lagoon to provide homes for small reef fish and invertebrates, and to encourage coral growth.

⚓ Many shore excursions include ecotourism components that benefit local communities and instruct tour guests on the wise use of natural resources.

⚓ More than 200 sea turtles have been nursed back to health and returned to their natural habitat by scientists at The Seas pavilion at Disney's Epcot theme park.

⚓ Dolphins, manatees, sea turtles, fish, and coral are some of the marine life protected and studied under the auspices of Disney's Worldwide Conservation Fund.

⚓ Each ship has its own Environmental Officer dedicated to environmental training, compliance, and waste management.

KEY WEST

The southernmost community in the continental U.S. and yet closer to Havana, Cuba, than it is to Miami, Key West is a charming blend of the best of Southern, Bahamian, Cuban, and Yankee food, architecture, and hospitality.

Discovered (along with the rest of Florida) by Ponce de León, and a favorite destination of fishermen, artists, and writers, this tiny piece of land was home for 30 years to Ernest Hemingway (who, among other works, penned *To Have and Have Not* and *For Whom the Bell Tolls* here). President Harry Truman had his "little White House" here, and Tennessee Williams, John Dos Passos, and Robert Frost found these friendly climes ideal for their creative and leisure liking. In fact, travelers can still visit Hemingway's Spanish Colonial-style house and lush gardens, and Truman's Little White House Museum.

By all means, take the tour train or the trolley to orient yourself, but once you've done that, Key West is best explored on foot—stop and admire the architecture—from Bahamian wooden gingerbread houses to those of New England sea captains—complete with widow's watch. The oldest house in Key West, circa 1829, was owned by a sea captain; you can still tour it and see its ship models, furnished dollhouse, and seafaring documents. For shoppers, galleries and crafts shops abound, as do lots and lots of places to buy T-shirts. Or do what most everyone else does and take to the water—be it by glass-bottom boat, semi-submersible, or kayak.

Sail, Kayak, and Snorkel Excursion
(5–5.5 hours; Ages 10 and up)

Get the best of all wet worlds in this day of adventure off Key West's shores. A sail aboard a two-masted schooner takes you through some mangrove-shrouded islands; then it's off the sailing ship and on to paddle your own kayak on an hour-long trip through unspoiled natural surroundings. Finally, don your snorkel gear (provided at no extra charge; instruction included, too) to discover the undersea wonders of Florida's most popular key. Welcome snacks at the end of the day include fresh fruit, chips, salsa, beverages, and more.

Some folks we spoke with were ardent snorkelers and admitted to loving most anything underwater; others were less enthusiastic, and said they would have preferred to have spent more time on the schooner.

⚓ Adults: $79 (ages 10 and above; not recommended for young children)
Departure Time: 12:20 P.M.

NEW PORT REPORT!

Disney Cruise Line recently started dropping anchor at two new Caribbean ports of call: Tortola and St. Croix. Though details on shore excursions were not final at press time, information will be available before you set sail. For the latest on the new port adventures, visit *www.disneycruise.com* or call 800-951-3532.

Back to Nature Kayak Tour
(3–3.5 hours; Ages 10 and up)

There's more to Florida than the beach. Climb aboard one of these double kayaks and paddle to the Wildlife Refuge; you'll be amazed at the number of (uninhabited) islands that are scattered along Florida Bay. You'll be in the company of a knowledgeable guide who will point out the wildlife and the natural wonders and answer any questions you may have. It's like looking for pirate treasure—without having to walk the plank. At the end of the sail, you'll be treated to a soft drink.

 Nature lovers will truly enjoy this tour. Looking at a bird is fine, but having a guide to tell you all about the bird and everything else you encounter makes this a wonderful—and peaceful—visit with Mother Nature.

⚓ Adults: $59 (ages 10 and above)
  Departure Times: 12:45 P.M.; 1:50 P.M.

White Knuckle Thrill Boat
(2 hours; Ages 8 and up)

They don't use the term "thrill" lightly here. Expect one wild ride when you board a high-performance jet boat. Hold on tight! We're talking 360-degree spins, sudden stops, and wild slides. The fun is shared by up to 11 other riders. The half hour of thrills is sandwiched by 20-minute bus transfers and 5-minute walks to and from the bus.

 The boat ride is fun, but the price is scary. The free drink is a nice touch, but if you're craving snackage, you'll have to buy it.

⚓ Adults: $65 (ages 10 and above)
  Children: $55 (ages 8–9)
  Departure Times: 12:55 P.M.; 2:05 P.M.

Key West Catamaran Sail & Snorkel Tour
(3–3.5 hours; Ages 5 and up)

If you're the seafaring sort, this is the best way to experience the magic of Key West. You'll enjoy a 3-hour sailing adventure that includes snorkeling amid vibrant coral and tropical fish. Snorkeling equipment and instruction are provided, as are beverages.

 Good marks were given by all the guests who took this tour.

⚓ Adults: $47 (ages 10 and above)
Children: $27 (ages 5–9)
Departure Time: 12:30 P.M.

Pirate Scavenger Hunt
(1.5 hours; All ages)

Avast, ye hearties, thar be a daily scavenger hunt a-happening at the Pirate Soul Museum, and you're invited to join in the fun. Guests reach the museum on foot (it's about a 10-minute walk) where they hunt solo or in groups (your choice). Guests who complete the hunt are rewarded with a swashbuckly bookmark.

 If you ask us, that is one expensive bookmark! But how often do you get to play in a pirate museum? For many kids the mere idea of that is priceless.

⚓ Adults: $23 (ages 10 and above)
Children: $13 (ages 5–9)
Under age 3: free
Departure Times: 1:50 P.M.; 2:40 P.M.

Pirate Soul Museum & Shipwreck Historeum
(2.5 hours; All ages)

Pirate enthusiasts step back in time and explore 17th-century Jamaica, where they gaze upon (and sometimes touch) artifacts and hear tales about the area's most notorious buccaneers. Energetic adventurers may ascend the 65-foot-high wrecking tower for a panoramic view of Key West.

Okay, so it's not Disney's Pirates of the Caribbean, but it's still cool. And the view from the tower is awesome.

⚓ Adults: $33 (ages 10 and above)
Children: $18 (ages 3–9)
Under age 3: free
Departure Time: 12:30 P.M.

Conch Republic Tour and Museum Package
(2–2.5 hours; All ages)

Hop aboard an open-air train for a drive-by tour of more than 100 of Key West's main attractions and historical sites. Once you've had your orientation, you'll be provided with admission media for self-guided visits to the Key West Aquarium and the Key West Shipwreck Historeum Museum.

While the tour gives a nice overview of the island, there is no opportunity to hop off and explore your favorite sites (a bummer for some). Neither museum earned raves from our crew. And our guide was gratuity-obsessed. Not cool. Though it was neat to see Ernest Hemingway's house.

⚓ Adults: $50 (ages 10 and above)
Children: $25 (ages 3–9)
Under age 3: free
Departure Time: 12:30 P.M.

Old Town Trolley or Conch Train Tour
(1–1.5 hours; All ages)

Train or trolley? Take your pick—either one will take you on a 60-minute tour in the southernmost city in the U.S. Expect to see 100 local points of interest, including attractions and historical sites, such as Ernest Hemingway's house, the famous Sloppy Joe's, and more.

We were a bit disappointed in this outing. First of all, the whirlwind pace left us frustrated. Why not a short stop at Hemingway's house, and how can they exclude the amazing Butterfly Conservatory?

⚓ Adults: $29 (ages 10 and above)
   Children: $14 (ages 3–9)
   Under age 3: free
   Departure Time: 1 P.M.

The Key West Butterfly & Nature Conservatory with Aquarium
(2.5 hours; All ages)

For those who crave serenity (now!), this excursion has your name on it. After a short walk and shuttle ride, guests enjoy a stroll through a tropical paradise. The climate-controlled environment is home to more than 50 species of butterfly, plus exotic and flowering plants, and cascading waterfalls. After the tour, guests are transported to the Key West Aquarium—the original tourist attraction in the Florida Keys.

We love this excursion. The Butterfly Conservatory is very interesting and serene. We overheard lots of "oohing" and "aahing" from kids and grown-ups alike. The aquarium delivers, too. They let you pet the sharks!

⚓ Adults: $36 (ages 10 and above)
   Children: $25 (ages 3–9)
   Under age 3: free
   Departure Time: 12:30 P.M.

Glass-Bottom Boat Tour on the Pride of Key West
(2.5–3 hours; All ages)

Perfectly named, the *Pride of Key West* is a 65-foot glass-bottom catamaran that gives passengers an incomparable view of the underwater world of the Keys. And comfort is key here, too: There are upper and lower sundecks, a large climate-controlled viewing area, and restrooms. A big plus is the narrated ecotour of North America's only living coral reef. Sit back, relax, and enjoy. Snacks and beverages are available to buy.

Comfort with a capital C is the key word to this Key tour. And the narration was a major plus.

⚓ Adults: $39 (ages 10 and above)
Children: $18 (ages 9 and under)
Departure Time: 1:45 P.M.

Presidents, Pirates, & Pioneers
(2 hours; Ages 3 and up)

Step back in time during this walking tour and discover the stories behind some of the city's most famous places, including the Shipwreck Historeum Museum and the Harry S. Truman Little White House. The tour concludes with complimentary conch fritters and bottled water. In all, expect to walk about 1.5 miles. Wheelchairs are permitted, but the Shipwreck Historeum is not wheelchair accessible.

This is a nice way to soak up a bit of history and get some exercise to boot. Wear comfortable walking shoes! A good tour guide makes all the difference in the world.

⚓ Adults: $35 (ages 10 and above)
Children: $23 (ages 3 to 9)

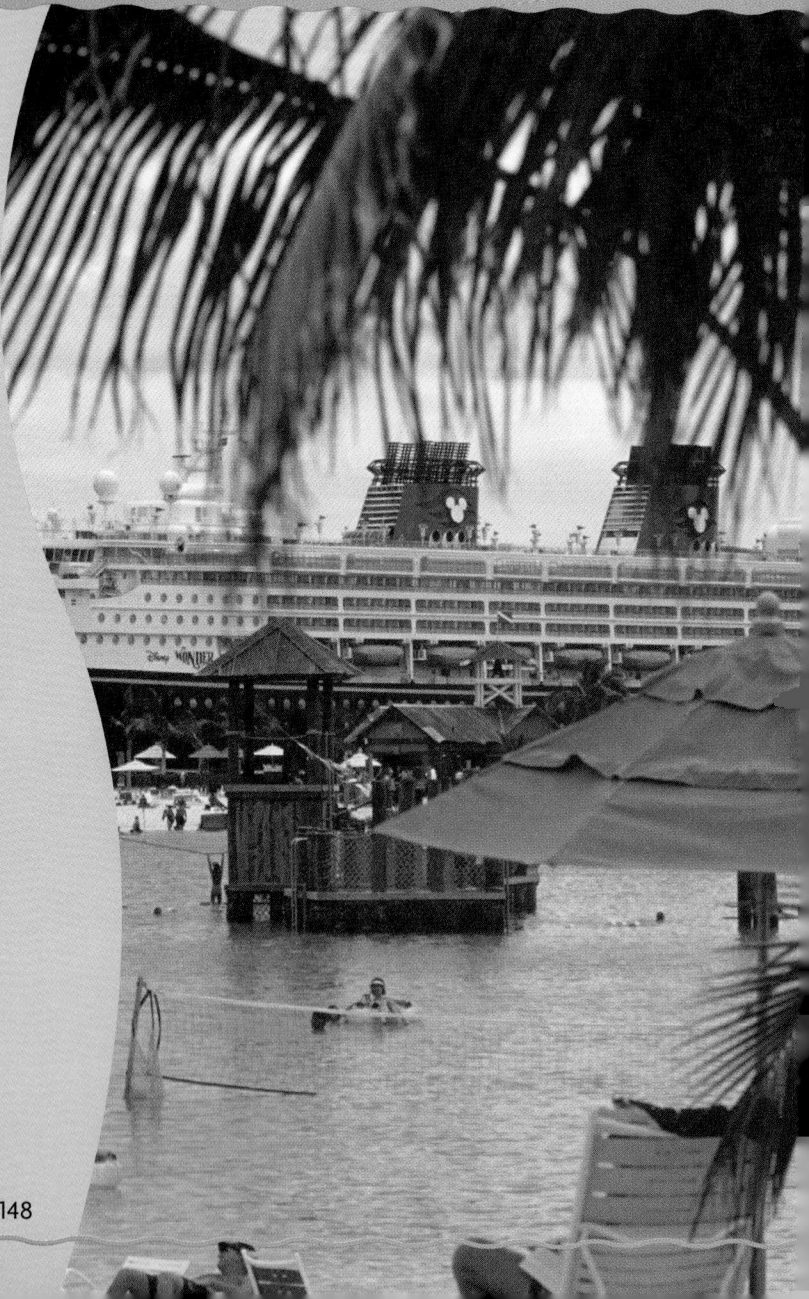
WONDER

Snorkel Lagoon Equipment Rental
(All day; Ages 5 and up)

You're on your own on this one: Pick up gear (at Gil's Fins and Boats) and put your face into the water of this 12-acre snorkel lagoon. Beginners can opt for Discover Trail, while more advanced water babies should follow the Explorer Trail. Snorkel awhile, rest on the beach, have some lunch, snorkel some more—the equipment rental is for the whole day. Snorkel, mask, fins, and vest included. Kids under 13 must be accompanied by an adult at all times.

Ideal environment for snorkel novices and small children. There's even an underwater Mickey Mouse to search for!

⚓ Adults: $25 (ages 10 and above)
Children: $10 (ages 5–9)
(Available all day)

Personal Watercraft Eco Tour
(1 hour; Ages 8 and up)

What's it like to live on Castaway Cay? Here's your chance to find out. Board a personal watercraft and listen as a guide shares stories about the island's marine life, ecology, and storied history. Then it's off to a second destination, where your guide will describe the colorful history and environment of the Bahamas. Water shoes or sandals are the preferred footwear. Eyeglass straps come in handy, too. Note that riders board from the water—dress appropriately.

Brief, but memorable. Lots of colorful photo ops. The boats are fun!

⚓ $95 for single riders;
$160 for double riders
Guests must be age 8 or older to ride; 18 and up to drive—16 with their parents' permission.
(Available all day)

Float/Tube Rentals
(All day; Ages 5 and up)

If doing absolutely nothing sounds good to you, rent a tube or float and bob in the gently rolling waves of a lagoon. The water is crystal clear and, best of all, rentals are good for the whole day! Children under 13 years of age must be accompanied by an adult. Don't forget the sunscreen.

What We Think

What's not to love? Take it all in—soon you're back in the real world.

⚓ Adults and children: $6 (ages 5 and above)
(Available All day)

154

Parasailing
(45 minutes, airborne 5–7 minutes; Ages 8 and up)

On this once-in-a-lifetime experience you can get a high-flying view of the world around you as you soar approximately 600 to 1,000 feet above Castaway Cay. You'll enjoy a whole new perspective of the landscape—and the boats that look more like bathtub toys. Although the entire flight lasts only five to seven minutes, the preparation for the adventure and landing encompasses about 45 minutes. It's an experience you won't soon forget. A couple of restrictions: guests must weigh more than 90 pounds, but must not exceed 375 pounds. Children under 13 must be accompanied by an adult.

One member of our hardy crew—at the tender age of 65—recently took to the skies on this aerial adventure. Not only did she live to tell about it, she said it was one of the most exhilarating experiences she'd ever had. And she told us . . . and she told us . . . and she's still telling us. Others found the experience a little scary, but thrilling. It really feels as though you're flying, but it's so gentle that you aren't always aware that you're moving. "Memorable" was the word from all who had their heads in the clouds.

⚓ Adults and children : $75 (ages 8 and above)
   Departure Times: Every 60 minutes, beginning
   at 10:30 A.M. on the *Disney Magic* and
   9 A.M. on the *Disney Wonder*

Banana Boat Ride
(15–20 minutes; Ages 8 and up)

Looks like a banana, floats like a boat. That's the fun of this short but wild ride on a yellow (of course) inflatable boat that skims the turquoise waters of the Bahamas while being pulled along by a Jet Ski (bananas need a little help getting around at sea). Expect to get dunked! Kids under 13 must be accompanied by an adult; and all guests must be able to swim.

 What We Think

Lots of fun in a short enough time so as not to keep you from enjoying the rest of the island. This is a great family (for those 8 years and older) experience.

⚓ Adults and children: $15 (ages 8 and up)
Departure Times: Every 30 minutes, beginning at 10 A.M. on the *Magic* and 8:50 A.M. on the *Wonder*

Bicycle Rental
(1 hour; All ages)

Don your helmet and enjoy a two-wheeled tour of Disney's private island. Bikes are available for rent by the hour, and there are child seats available for the little ones. Children must be able to ride a two-wheel bike and are required to wear helmets.

 What We Heard

This was an excellent family experience for all. Little ones sat at the rear of grown-ups' bikes, while older children had their own bikes. The roads aren't the smoothest, but everyone said that it was a fun hour's diversion.

⚓ Adults and children: $6 per hour (All day)

Castaway Cay Getaway Package

(Ages 5 and up)

For active folks who want to snorkel and bike about this Disney isle, here's an all-inclusive-priced package that lets you frolic til your heart's content. You'll receive snorkeling equipment and float rental for the day, plus a one-hour bicycle rental. Children under 13 must be accompanied by an adult.

What We Think

Since it's pretty much a given that you'll want to snorkel, float, and splash in the ocean, or pedal about the island, the only real question to ask yourself is: Will I (and my family) want to do all three? If the answer is an enthusiastic yes, then we say go for it!

⚓ Adults: $32 (ages 10 and above)
   Children: $16 (ages 5–9)
   (All day)

The Wild Side
(4 hours; Ages 13–17)

Attention, teens! Here's an adventure designed exclusively for you. Venture into uncharted territory as you explore the wild side of the island where you can snorkel, bike-ride, and sea-kayak on your own. No moms, dads, or baby brothers and sisters here.

What We Heard

The teens who came back from this trip had nothing but good things to say about it; it was a special time to spend with old friends and new, and enjoy some grown-up hours away from parents and siblings. Awesome!

⚓ Teens: $35 (13–17 only)
　 Departure Times:
　 9 A.M. *Magic*;
　 8:20 A.M. *Wonder*

Boat Rental
(4 hours; Ages 5 and up)

For those who can't get enough of the Bahamian waters, a variety of boats are available for rent at Gil's Fins and Boats. All craft are subject to availability. They can't be reserved in advance— it's all walk-up rental only. Children under 13 must be accompanied by an adult. All prices are for a half-hour rental, per person:

Paddleboats: 2-seater $8; 4-seater $10. Sea Kayak: 1-seater $8; 2-seater $10. Aqua Fin: $15. Aqua Trike: $15. Hobie Cat: $18.

What We Think

Your choice. It's all here. Paddle (or pedal) to your heart's content.

⚓ Adults and children: $8–$18
　 per half hour
　 (All day)

Grouper Game Pavilion
(All ages)

Need a break from the sun? We've got just the place for you—Castaway Cay's Grouper Game Room. Located near the volleyball nets and the sports beach, it is a *shaded* game room and recreation area where guests of all ages can play table tennis, basketball, shuffleboard, foosball, giant checkers, a game of pool, and more. Happy news for Mom and Dad: These are fun and *free* activities.

 A surefire hit with kids, we've noticed more than a few grown-ups enjoying themselves in these parts. Table tennis, anyone?

⚓ Adults: Free
  Children: Free
  (All day)

PRACTICAL PACKAGE DEALS

Too lazy to take pictures? Think about springing for the Photography Package. For one lump sum, pictures of your family with Mickey, Minnie, Chip and Dale, and even Cinderella can grace your family photo album without your clicking a finger.

Wine lovers should be aware of Disney's wine packages; when you prepay for several bottles at a time, you save big bucks.

Beer drinkers may purchase a "refillable mug," good for discount suds throughout the cruise.

HOT TIP

It's best to book your desired shore excursions before you leave home, since many of the most popular tours can be full by the time you get onboard. You can still make changes or cancel tours up to 3 days prior to cruise departure date. Excursions may be booked up to 75 days in advance. (Repeat guests can reserve 90 days ahead, and Concierge guests can do so 105 days prior to sailing.)

Extreme Getaway Package
(Ages 5 and up)

As with the Castaway Cay Getaway Package, this is not for lazy beach bums. The all-inclusive deal lets you have it all (well, most of it!) in a single day. You'll receive snorkeling equipment and float rental for the day, a one-hour stingray encounter (courtesy of the island's own Castaway Ray), plus a one-hour bicycle rental. And, yes, there will be some time for you to snooze in the sun, too! Children under 13 must be accompanied by an adult.

Too much of a good thing? Nah. You simply can't get enough of Castaway Cay. We find this package "extreme"-ly enjoyable.

⚓ Adults: $54 (ages 10 and above)
Children: $39 (ages 5–9)
(All day)

Castaway Ray's Stingray Adventure
(1 hour; Ages 5 and up)

Get up close and personal with Southern stingrays in Castaway Cay's private lagoon. (Don't worry, they can't sting.) The guided encounter (a human "Ray" is your guide) includes a background session about these interesting sea creatures and snorkel instruction. The adventure culminates with a chance to feed, touch, and swim with the rays.

We know every minute on Castaway Cay is precious, but this is an hour well spent. We'll play with the rays any day.

⚓ Adults: $35 (ages 10 and above)
   Children: $29 (ages 5–9)
   (Available all day)

NASSAU

Is it really better in the Bahamas? That depends on who you ask! Within this island paradise, you will find places to shop, swim, snorkel, sail, gamble, and sip a cool, refreshing beverage while looking out over a turquoise blue ocean. (Some say the shopping district is sensational, others find it uninspired—different strokes for different folks.)

Beaches are plentiful, but for those who like to venture beyond the sand, there are places here where goats outnumber TV sets, and where not-so-smooth roads and ferries that are off schedule more than on will take you to the "true" Bahamas—where Bahamians do their traditional dance, the *junkanoo,* and *goombay* music fills the air. This is where you can sample some

authentic island cooking (lots of grouper, lobster, conch, and johnnycakes) and really take a turn at going native, if only for a few hours.

There are actually about 200 islands and some 2,000 cays (pronounced *keys*) in the Bahamas, all scattered across 100,000 square miles of the Atlantic Ocean. The adventures that are described on the following pages are available to you in Nassau, the island nation's capital. Aside from its divine diving rich in shipwrecks, there is much more to see in the Bahamas—be it lush gardens and waterfalls, or Victorian mansions and 17th-century Georgian buildings. The good news is that, for the most part, the island's pride in its heritage is reflected in the way it is maintained.

Discover Atlantis
(2–5 hours; All ages)

This is the perfect place to put your imagination to work as you immerse yourself in the legend of the lost city of Atlantis. A 20-minute, narrated bus tour drops you off a short distance from the Atlantis resort. Here's where the real fun begins: A guided voyage through the attraction, Discover Atlantis, reveals more than 120,000 fish representing 150 species, and re-creates the lost city. You will get an interesting look at life in the ocean's depths. Return bus transportation is included and available every half hour from 1 P.M. to 5:30 P.M. After this time, you will need to take a taxi (additional cost) back to the ship before departure.

NOTE: There's lots of walking involved with this tour. Wear comfortable shoes.

This was a tour that featured a little bit of everything—a lot of truth, a little fiction, and an informed guide who asked only that you bring along your imagination. But . . . some people felt that they could have done as well getting to Atlantis without an excursion.

Adults: $39 (ages 10 and above)
Children: $26 (ages 3–9)
Under age 3: free
Departure Times: 11 A.M.; 1 P.M.

HOT TIP

If you've got kids in tow, be sure to ask your tour director about potential pit stops *before* the tour begins.

Atlantis Beach Day
(4–7 hours; All ages)

Here's a full-day adventure that begins with a 20-minute bus ride through the historic area of Nassau's Paradise Island, where you'll be dropped off at the nearby Atlantis resort. Upon arrival, guests get a beach chair and towel and someone to escort them to a reserved location on the beach to bask in the sun and surf. Have lunch at the Dive In snack bar (coupon provided), and the day is yours to spend as you like. Enjoy gaming at the casino, shopping at a variety of unique stores, or visiting Discover Atlantis, a special marine habitat that's home to more than 120,000 fish representing 150 species. Return bus transportation is included and available until 5:30 P.M. After this time, you will need to take a taxi (at additional cost) back to the ship.

NOTE: This excursion involves extensive walking. Wear comfortable shoes. Use of the pools and waterslides is not included.

As with the Discover Atlantis tour (page 164), this was a good way to learn about Atlantis and sea life, but on this tour you also have time to lie on the beach. Some people were disappointed that many of the amenities of Atlantis were not included—especially access to the better part of the beach. One couple thought it would have been better to rent a room at the Atlantis for the day and get everything included. We think that's going a bit far, but as they say, different strokes . . .

⚓ Adults: $65 (ages 10 and above)
Children: $47 (ages 9 and under)
Departure Time: 9 A.M.

Nassau Dolphin Encounter
(4–4.5 hours; Ages 3 and up)

First of all—do *not* forget your camera! You will definitely want to preserve images of you and your crew interacting with some of the sea's friendliest creatures. The adventure begins with a 30-minute educational orientation followed by a 5- to 8-minute nose-to-snout meeting. (Water is only waist-deep for this "meeting.") Note that this excursion does not include a beach experience. Lunch items are available for purchase, as are professional photos and videos of the experience. It takes about an hour to get to and from the dolphin lagoon (20 minutes of walking, 40 on the ferry).

We'll admit it: We find petting dolphins to be one of the cooler experiences life has to offer. Most kids loved this one, too, although one little boy was frightened. A photographer was there to capture the moment every time a dolphin came close. (Other items available for purchase include 8 x 10 and wallet-size photos, postcards, videos, and framed photographs.)

⚓ Adults: $99 (ages 10 and above)
Children: $84 (ages 3–9)
Departure Time: 9:15 A.M.

Nassau City Tour
(2 hours; All ages)

See the charms of this port city in the comfort of an air-conditioned van. The guided tour includes the facts and fiction, and the history and the lore that are the essence of Nassau. You will visit historic buildings, stop at significant sites and famous homes, and see such memorable landmarks as Fort Charlotte, Fort Fincastle and the Water Tower, and the Queen's Staircase. Shopper's alert: Ask the driver to end your tour at the famous Straw Market.

A bit of a disappointment. "We should have gone to the beach." Some found the town (at least the shopping areas) "tacky at best," although we find the pastel-colored buildings charming.

Adults: $23 (ages 10 and above)
Children: $18 (ages 3–9); under age 3: free
Departure Time: 10 A.M.

Scuba Dive Adventure at Stuart Cove
(4.5–5 hours; Ages 12 and up)

For experienced divers only (you must present a certification card); this is your chance to have an in-depth look at the natural reefs and tropical fish found in the waters of the Bahamas. Once on board the dive boat (it's about a 45-minute bus ride to get there), you'll be briefed on safety instructions en route to the dive site near New Providence Island. Weather and tidal conditions permitting, the first of two dives is a reef wall dive of 40–80 feet; the second is a reef or wreck dive of 25–50 feet. An insured P.A.D.I. dive master or instructor comes along for the dives. Guests under 17 must be accompanied by a parent or guardian.

What We Think

If you're into scuba diving, this tour doesn't disappoint. The fish and reefs are as advertised . . . magnificent!

⚓ Adults: $99 (ages 12 and above;
   not recommended for younger children)
   Departure Time: 11:45 A.M.

Atlantis Aquaventure
(5–8 hours; All ages)

The excursion begins with a 25-minute bus ride and an escorted walk (about 20 minutes) to the 63-acre water park at the Atlantis resort. Following a guided tour of an underwater aquarium, you're free to enjoy the waterslides, river rapids, pools, and more. Water bikes, kayaks, and snorkel equipment may be rented. A light lunch is included. You'll have access to a beach, shopping, and a casino, too. Guests must be at least 48 inches tall to ride the waterslides. Swim diapers are a must for babies.

Water park fans will not be disappointed (well, unless the weather is crummy). It's a bit of a splurge, but we're not complaining. (Yeah, we love water parks.)

⚓ Adults: $155 (ages 10 and above)
   Children: $105 (ages 5–9)
   Under age 3: Free

Atlantis Dolphin Cay & Aquaventure
(6–8 hours; Ages 3 and up)

Take the tour at left and toss in an educational encounter with dolphins, and you have an idea of what this day is all about. Dolphin Cay is an 11-acre state-of-the-art home to more than 20 of the lovable creatures. After a tour of the marine habitat, a guide takes you to Dolphin Cay and offers an overview of dolphin behaviors. Then it's time to don a wetsuit and mingle with the majestic mammals. Expect to bond for about 30 minutes. Before your swimsuit has time to dry, you'll be making a splash at the Aquaventure water park.

If budget's not an issue, this is a great experience for the whole family. It's a long day, but a memorable one.

⚓ Adults: $285 (ages 10 and above)
   Children: $245 (ages 3 and up)

Blackbeard's Cay Stingray & Beach Adventure

(4.5–5 hours; Ages 3 and up)

The population of the underwater "Stingray Adventure" will be glad to mingle with you on this combination tour. First, a boat brings you to Blackbeard's Cay, where the fun begins. The reason we call this a combination tour is that you can interact with these fascinating and friendly creatures and then unwind on the beach and enjoy lunch (sandwiches, chips, and soft drink; no extra charge) before heading back to the ship. Remember to wear swimsuits and sunscreen.

What We Think

Stingray lovers that we are, we adore this tour. The area is beautiful, too. Relaxing on the beach afterward was a perfect ending to the day.

⚓ Adults: $47 (ages 10 and above)
   Children: $35 (ages 3–9)
   Departure Time: 9:45 A.M.

Ardastra Gardens and City Tour
(2.5 hours; All ages)

Expect a little bit of this and a little bit of that on this nature-history tour. You'll visit the tropical Gardens of Ardastra, where you can see the world-famous marching flamingos strut their stuff, feed beautiful lory parrots by hand, and view the largest collection of Bahamian land animals in the world. Then board a bus for a narrated city tour. Stops include many of Nassau's historical points of interest, such as Fort Fincastle, the Water Tower, and the Queen's Staircase.

What We Think

For us, the best part of the day was feeding the parrots, but there's so much else to see that you may find yourself short on time when you get to them. The birds are very tame, and feeding them is great fun. The flamingo show is good, and here's where you get to have your picture taken—standing on one leg, of course. The staff is very friendly and knowledgeable, and the bus tour was interesting. The only downside: By the time we got back to the port most of the souvenir stands were closed.

⚓ Adults: $38 (ages 10 and above)
   Children: $29 (ages 3–9); under age 3: free
   Departure Time: 12:45 P.M.

ST. MAARTEN

Some call it St. Maarten, while others insist it's St. Martin. And they're both right. During the 1600s, after centuries of battles over dominance, Spain bowed out and the deadlocked Dutch and French agreed to disagree and split this small island in half—well, not quite half: The French got 21 square miles and the Dutch 16. (Legends abound as to why, but our favorite is that the two countries decided to claim their territory by conducting a race around the island and the French won.)

St. Maarten—the Dutch side of the island, and one of the world's only land masses owned by two countries—is the lively sector, while St. Martin—the bucolic French side, larger but more serene, attracts visitors who crave peace and tranquillity—

with some gourmet food thrown in for good measure. Both sides boast abundant beaches and sparkling waters. Shoppers enjoy Philipsburg's no-tax-on-imported-goods policy. Lots of shops are downright tacky, but with a little effort you can manage to part with some green stuff during your stay. And, of course, there's gambling. Casinos line the area by the pier and most of the Dutch-side hotels offer games of chance. The French, meanwhile, have bouillabaisse and onion soup. So it's possible to swim anywhere, have a meal on either side of the island, and either go to a club in Marigot (the French capital) or play the slots on the Dutch side. Whatever you choose, the cards are stacked in your favor on this *très* continental isle.

175

Pinel Island Snorkel Tour
(3.5 hours; Ages 5 and up)

This tour offers guests the chance to visit the French side of the island (St. Martin) and sail away to a private getaway for snorkeling and beach fun. The day begins with a bus tour from the ship to the northeast French coast. From there you board a water taxi for the short ride to Pinel Island, a spit of land off the coast. Snorkeling instruction and equipment are available, and then it's snorkel time. The rewards are a fascinating world of coral reefs and an amazingly colorful array of tropical fish. Afterward, you can get a soft drink and catch some rays, or visit the boutiques—and see what damage can be done by exploring the deepest reaches of your wallet!

What We Think

First, it was a great chance to see the French side of the island; second, the snorkeling was great; third—and best of all to some of us—the shopping was excellent.

⚓ Adults: $37 (ages 10 and above)
Children: $31 (ages 5–9)
Departure Time: 8 A.M.

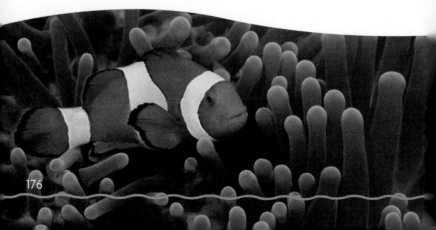

Shipwreck Cove Snorkel Tour
(3.5 hours; Ages 8 and up)

For serious snorkelers (beginners can try their fins here, but this tour is not recommended for non-swimmers), this is quite possibly as good as it gets. A spectacular look at the world under your mask, this undersea adventure is rich in sunken ships, coral reefs, and a gazillion colorful fish that you can actually hand-feed. Equipment and refreshments are provided.

This experience was everything we hoped for and more. Our group consisted of dedicated snorkelers, the weather couldn't have been better, and . . . need we say more?

⚓ Adults: $41
(ages 10 and above)
Children: $34
(ages 8–9)
Departure Time: 1 P.M.

Golden Eagle Catamaran
(4 hours; Ages 5 and up)

The beautiful Caribbean is yours for the swimming—or snorkeling (equipment provided) or sunbathing—on a relaxing ride that concludes with pastries and an open bar.

A pleasant way to pass the time in the Caribbean. It was very laid-back, and if that's what you yearn for, this is for you.

⚓ Adults: $71 (ages 10 and above)
Children: $41 (ages 5–9)
Departure Times: 7:45 A.M.; 1 P.M.

"Bubba" Fishing
(4–4.5 hours; Ages 6 and up)

A family-friendly, catch-and-release experience, this trip involves a 45-minute cruise to and from the fishing spot. Everyone is supplied with rods, reels, bait, and assistance. Total fishing time is about two hours. Soft drinks are included. In case you were wondering, *Bubba* is the name of the boat.

Nice for novices and seasoned fisher-folk alike, though younger anglers may get antsy.

⚓ Adults: $90 (ages 10 and above)
   Children: $77 (ages 6–9)
   Departure Time: 8:30 A.M.

Island Drive and Explorer Cruise
(4 hours; All ages)

Here you can enjoy the best of all worlds, visit Simpsons Bay Lagoon, and then board the *Explorer* for a half-hour cruise to Marigot, the island's French capital. Sightsee and shop, and then take the scenic return to Philipsburg, the Dutch capital, where you can do some more sightseeing and shopping. Too history-heavy? Not a bit. Expensive? Only if you can't resist the shopping scene. Let your budget—and your willpower—be your guide.

This was interesting—if you're into learning about island history. If you'd rather hit the beach, look elsewhere. We loved the French side, although Philipsburg is not without its charms.

⚓ Adults: $47 (ages 10 and above)
   Children: $24 (ages 9 and under)
   Departure Time: 1:15 P.M.

12-Metre Regatta
(3 hours; Ages 12 and up)

On this exciting sail, the closest thing to being a participant in an America's Cup race, you can be as much a part of the crew as you like, or just sit back and enjoy while others do the work. "Crew members"—that's *you*—are trained in everything from trimming a sail, to punching a stopwatch to grinding a winch. It's so authentic that the fleet here includes the 1987 America's Cup winner, Dennis Conner's *Stars & Stripes US-55*. Sailing experience isn't required, but it can certainly enhance your enjoyment of the trip.

 What We Heard

If you love boating, don't miss this experience. Lots of group members actually participated in the working of the ship; others just sat back and watched. Your call.

⚓ Adults: $75 (ages 12 and above;
not recommended for younger children)
Departure Time: 8:15 A.M.

French Riviera Beach Rendezvous
(5 hours; All ages)

Orient Bay, called "the French Riviera of the Caribbean," is where lounging on your own specially reserved beach chair on a mile-and-a-half white sand beach and enjoying lunch and cool drinks amid coconut palms and lush sea grapes is *de rigeur*. On the way to the beach, your guide will give you a brief history of the whole island—but this outing is really about the beach, the beach, and nothing but the beach. Note that nude or topless bathing may occur.

It's a beautiful beach—the sand, the gentle waves, the total relaxation.

⚓ Adults: $57 (ages 10 and above)
   Children: $40 (ages 3–9)
   Under age 3: free
   Departure Time: 9:45 A.M.

Tiki Hut Snorkel
(2–6 hours; Ages 6 and up)

The *Tiki Hut* is actually a boat. A floating lounge, if you will. One that will serve you food and drink (for a fee) in between dips into the calm waters of a sheltered cove. Snorkeling equipment and instruction are provided. Hourly tenders (water taxis) are available back to the ship or downtown. It's about a 15-minute trip.

We are drawn to the kitschy concept. A treat for grown-ups, it seems a bit splurgy for young kids—they are less likely to be charmed by the tiki-rific-ness and more likely to have their fill of snorkeling long before the 6-hour limit.

⚓ Adults: $59 (ages 10 and above)
   Children: $42 (ages 6–9)
   Departure Times: 8:55 A.M.; 12:55 P.M.

Under 2 Flags Island Tour
(3 hours; All ages)

As different as their European counterparts, the French and Dutch parts of this island are well worth exploring. Here's an opportunity to see the best of both worlds on a scenic narrated bus tour, which includes a stop at Marigot, the French capital, for shopping and exploring the local markets—or perhaps a coffee at a café?

This was a good chance to see and learn about this bi-national island. Our guide was first-rate, and the air-conditioned bus was comfortable (try to get a seat up front; the views are much better). We enjoyed the French side of the island more than the Dutch side; the architecture is prettier, the restaurants excellent—though we steered clear of the cockfighting (yikes!). We did some shopping in Marigot. The open-air market is rife with island shirts and dresses, plus some jewelry and assorted souvenirs. If you're really into it, you can let the bus go and take a taxi back to the ship.

⚓ Adults: $22 (ages 10 and above)
   Children: $17 (ages 3–9); under age 3: free
   Departure Time: 8:45 A.M.

St. Maarten Island and Butterfly Farm Tour
(3.5 hours; All ages)

Originating in Philipsburg, this narrated bus tour offers stunning scenery and, best of all, a visit to a butterfly farm on the island's French side. Once you've had your fill of fluttery creatures you can fritter away time in Marigot, where markets, cafés, and duty-free shops are at your disposal.

 A mom and daughter who took this tour enjoyed it, but agreed with others in observing that it was a bit too long—definitely not worth four hours of potential beach time.

⚓ Adults: $34 (ages 10 and above)
   Children: $28 (ages 3–9)
   Under age 3: free
   Departure Time: 8 A.M.

Certified Scuba Dive
(4.5 hours; Ages 12 and up)

A memorable underwater adventure off these Caribbean shores awaits certified divers as they don their gear and go nose-to-nose with colorful coral and exotic fish. Not for landlubbers, this fish story is limited to those who have a diving certification card and have completed at least one dive in the last two years.

 Excellent! From top to bottom and back again.

⚓ Adults: $94 (ages 12 and above; not appropriate for younger children)
   Departure Time: 8:50 A.M.

See and Sea Island Tour
(3.5 hours; All ages)

Everything worth seeing on land and sea can be yours on this eclectic tour. The action begins with a narrated bus trip to Grand Case, during which you can appreciate the beauty of the landscape. The bus tour is followed by a trip aboard the semi-submarine *Seaworld Explorer*, which lets you spy on sea creatures. Finally, the day ends with a visit to the quaint French town of Marigot, where cafés and shopping abound.

This tour had its heart in the right place, but its timing was way off: too little time to do much of anything anywhere.

⚓ Adults: $51 (ages 10 and above)
Children: $36 (ages 9 and under)
Departure Times: 8:15 A.M.; 1:15 P.M.

Seaworld Explorer– Coral Reef Exploration
(2.5 hours; Ages 3 and up)

Here's your chance to spy on sea creatures without getting the least bit water-logged. A 45-minute voyage on the semi-submarine *Seaworld Explorer* lets guests ooh and aah at aquatic life in its natural habitat *and* when some of it's brought aboard the vessel, courtesy of a skilled diver-sea critter wrangler. Beverages are included, but you may want to pack a snack. Unfortunately, wheelchairs cannot be accommodated aboard the vessel.

The commute-time to fun-time ratio is a bit lopsided for our taste. But if you fancy yourself a semi-sub fan, it just may make your day. Claustrophobes, however, should sit this one out.

⚓ Adults: $39 (ages 10 and above)
Children: $29 (ages 3–9)
Departure Time: 11 A.M.

Anguilla Dolphin Encounter
(7–7.5 hours; Ages 5 and up)

We don't know which part of this tour is best: Is it the opportunity to feed, photograph (don't forget your camera), or frolic with dolphins? All of the above, of course. A barbecue lunch is served at Meads Bay. If time allows, you can hang at the beach.

Let's put it this way—we loved Anguilla, loved the dolphins, didn't love the food. Two out of three isn't bad—except that the hefty price exceeded the actual pleasure.

⚓ Adults: $188 (ages 10 and up)
Children: $162 (ages 5–9)
Departure Times: 7:30 A.M.;
11:30 A.M.

Observer: Anguilla Dolphin Encounter
(7–7.5 hours; Ages 3 and up)

Landlubbers, do not despair: You can accompany a friend or family member and watch—staying completely dry—as they interact with the dolphins. You can join them for lunch and a little beach time, too.

The non-swimmers we spoke with gave this a thumbs-up. The price tag is steep, but it's nice to have the chance to "ride along."

⚓ Adults: $129 (ages 10 and up)
Children: $101 (ages 3–9)
Departure Time: 7:30 A.M.

Rhino Rider and Snorkeling Adventure
(3.5 hours; Ages 10 and up)

Here's a chance to pilot your own boat—actually a two-person inflatable raft—across Simpson Bay Lagoon and take in the amazing coastline views. Chase that by setting out to sea and enjoying the spectacular sights of Marigot and Fort St. Louis. And that's not all: Before returning to the lagoon you can snorkel at one of the island's prime watering spots and relax at one of St. Maarten's best-known watering holes (the first beverage is included).

We had fun, but would have preferred a little more snorkeling and a little less rafting. But that's just us.

⚓ Adults: $84 per guest with a maximum of two in a boat, with a 440-pound combined weight limit (ages 10 and above). Guests must be 18 or older to drive the Rhino Rider. Departure Times: 7:45 A.M.; 1:45 P.M.

Afternoon Beach Bash
(3.5–4 hours; All ages)

It takes about 30 minutes to reach Orient Bay by bus, but the payoff for your patience is about two full hours of fun in the sun on one of the Caribbean's best beaches. Fruit punch and rum punch are free-flowing (literally—there's no charge), while water sports equipment, parasailing, hair-braiding, and massages are available for an extra charge. Food and additional beverages may be purchased at any of the full-service restaurants or beach bars. Note that nudity or topless bathing may be encountered.

All in all, an enjoyable beach day—and an excellent value. Not for the modest (see above note!).

⚓ Adults: $37 (ages 10 and up)
Children: $20 (ages 3–9)
Departure Time: 1:45 P.M.

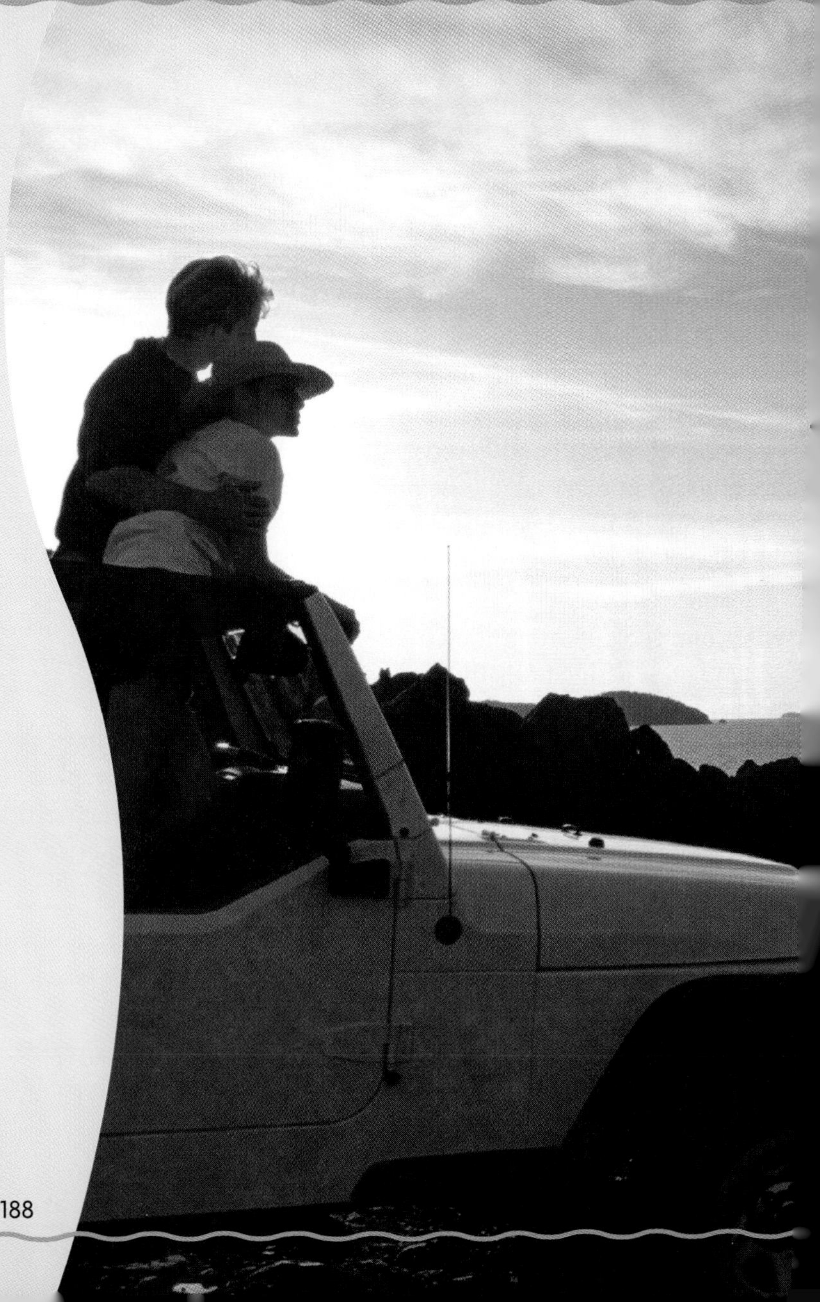

ST. THOMAS/ST. JOHN

Among the world's most popular cruise destinations, these two islands—just 20 minutes yet a world away from each other—were discovered by Christopher Columbus in 1493, on his second journey to the New World. St. Thomas is a mere 32 square miles; St. John, its smaller sibling, is just 19 square miles.

St. Thomas has weathered its fair share of hurricane damage in the not-too-distant past but has bounced back in dramatic fashion. Rebuilt and revitalized, it has become a gathering spot for ships, large, larger, and largest (some might say too many), to drop anchor. Rightfully claiming to have one of the world's most beautiful beaches, it's a destination for that alone. Yet there is more—much more—to the island than the beach. The duty-free shopping is possibly second to none, with the streets of Charlotte Amalie overflowing with jewelry shops and galleries; it's also a place to pick up such local island souvenirs as scrimshaw, sculpture, dolls, ceramics, and basketry. Actually, you could easily spend an entire day (or days) shopping here.

A short ferry ride away, St. John is the laid-back sibling, boasting hiking trails, more than three dozen white-coral sand coves, and replete with more flowers and ferns, butterflies and birds than would fit into the best dreamer's imaginings. As you might imagine, nature rules here, and it is a kingdom anyone—bird or human—would be proud to call their own.

St. John Trunk Bay Beach and Snorkel Tour
(5 hours; Ages 5 and up)

Embrace the charm of St. John on this land and sea tour that shows off the splendor of Trunk Bay Beach. Whether you opt to sunbathe or snorkel (equipment provided), life is truly a beach here.

It's as good as it gets. Having five hours to do just as you please is wonderful; the snorkeling was first-rate, too.

⚓ Adults: $48 (ages 10 and above)
   Children: $34 (ages 5–9)
   Departure Time: 7:40 A.M.

St. John Island Tour
(5–5.5 hours; All ages)

A scenic boat ride from St. Thomas brings you to the unspoiled island of St. John, where you board an open safari bus that tools around the island—including a stop at the Annaberg Ruins (with its abandoned plantation house and sugar mill)—and affords breathtaking views of neighboring islands.

We didn't hear great things about this tour. Most folks were wishing they were on the beach.

⚓ Adults: $42 (ages 10 and above)
Children: $31 (ages 9 and under)
Departure Time: 7:40 A.M.

St. John Eco Hike
(5 hours; Ages 6 and up)

You'll put 1.2 miles on your tennis or hiking shoes as you march through the lush forests of Cruz Bay. Scenic Lind Point Lookout and Honeymoon Beach are on the tour, too. Happily, there's plenty of time for swimming before heading to the Caneel Bay Plantation.

This gets a big thumbs-up from all of us. The scenery was amazing, the swimming superb, and the plantation was an excellent end-of-day treat.

⚓ Adults: $60 (ages 10 and above)
Children: $50 (ages 6–9)
Departure Time: 7:40 A.M.

191

Butterfly Secrets & Mountain Views
(2.5–3 hours; All ages)

After an hour-long scenic journey to Mountain Top (complete with a photo op stop overlooking Magens Bay Beach and a visit to a souvenir shop), you'll immerse yourself in the wonderful world of butterflies. A guide will regale you with stories while hundreds of the colorful insects flutter about. Do not forget the camera. Wheelchairs must be manual and collapsible.

 What's not to love about a swirling swarm of beautiful butterflies? The bus ride is a bit long, and we didn't need the shopping stop, but the butterfly farm certainly was special.

⚓ Adults: $35 (ages 10 and above)
  Children: $24 (ages 3–9)
  Under age 3: free

Magens Bay Beach Break
(4.5 hours; All ages)

Spend time enjoying the laid-back lifestyle of the Caribbean at St. Thomas's premier beach (in fact, it's considered one of the most beautiful beaches in the world), where you can swim and sunbathe (beach chairs available on a first-come, first-served basis). Floats and water toys may be rented; beverages, snacks, and lunch items may be purchased. Water is free. It takes about 25 minutes to get to and from the beach (via bus).

 Beach bums like us delight over this glorious day of rest and relaxation.

⚓ Adults: $44
  (ages 10 and above)
  Children: $33 (ages 3–9)
  Under age 3: free
  Departure Time: 9 A.M.

5-Star St. John Snorkel and Beach Adventure
(4 hours; Ages 5 and up)

This is one of our favorite tours (and everybody else's, too). After you board the 115-foot *Leylon Sneed* you will sail from St. Thomas to Trunk Bay, in St. John. Later, you'll snorkel at St. John National Park (instruction and equipment provided), swim and sunbathe, and sip a rum or fruit punch. Sound sweet? It is.

 Look at everything said above and double it. We loved this day.

⚓ Adults: $48 (ages 10 and above)
Children: $34 (ages 5–9)
Departure Time: 7:40 A.M.

Atlantis Submarine Adventure
(2.5–3 hours; Ages 4 and up)

Come face-to-face with the various creatures of the deep without even getting wet aboard *Atlantis XV*, the world's newest and most advanced passenger submarine. The narrated journey from St. Thomas reaches depths of up to 90 feet—colorful, exotic fish, sponge gardens, and coral formations are there for the viewing.

Note that guests must be at least 36 inches tall to participate.

 A good outing for nonclaustrophobes. The guide did a good job of educating the passengers. Most folks we spoke with gave it high marks.

⚓ Adults: $89 (ages 10 and above)
Children: $57 (ages 4–9)
Departure Times: 8:30 A.M.;
9:30 A.M.; 10:30 A.M.; 12:30 P.M.

Butterfly Anytime
(All day; All ages)

Just a 3-minute stroll from the pier (and your ship), this tranquil Butterfly Farm is pleasant for all ages (provided, of course, that you enjoy butterfly-watching). A friendly guide will help you discover the fascinating life cycle of the winged insect—from caterpillar to flying marvel. Don't be surprised if one of the hundreds of fluttering butterflies stops to perch on your head. And be gentle!

Butterflies are pretty. This is our preferred way to visit them (it's better than the tour on page 192).

⚓ Adults: $15
  (ages 10 and above)
  Children: $9 (ages 3–9)
  Under age 3: free
  Farm Opening Time: 9 A.M.

Doubloon Sail and Snorkel Tour
(3.5 hours; Ages 5 and up)

Ahoy, matey! You'll feel as though you've stepped back in time when you board the 65-foot schooner *Doubloon*. The treasures to be found on this sail from St. Thomas are the memories you get to take home with you—and at Turtle Cove at Buck Island, you'll also have time to snorkel (equipment and beverages provided).

Note that no food is served onboard, so take a snack (no fresh fruit). Our guide was meticulous in informing us about the snorkeling, insisting that we wear life jackets and getting into the water with us to point out the giant sea turtles below. The captain sells souvenir Doubloon T-shirts, so you might want to bring some cash.

⚓ Adults: $49 (ages 10 and above)
  Children: $32 (ages 5–9)
  Departure Times: 8:15 A.M.;
  12:15 P.M.

St. John Barefoot Sail and Snorkel
(4.5 hours; Ages 5 and up)

Best of land and sea, this excursion includes a scenic drive to La Vida Marina and a sail on the *Allure* to one of St. John's beautiful white-sand beaches. There's time for snorkeling (equipment is provided), swimming, sunbathing—all that good stuff.

People on this outing loved everything about it and had a hard time tearing themselves away from the beach.

⚓ Adults: $75 (ages 10 and above)
　Children: $55 (ages 5–9)
　Departure Time: 7:45 A.M.

St. Thomas Island Tour
(2.5 hours; All ages)

To fully absorb the natural beauty of the island, take this open-air (wear a hat for sun protection) safari bus ride—and be sure to bring your camera. Photo ops abound at almost every turn, especially when you reach Mountain Top, the highest point on the island.

If you've never been here before, this is a great way to see the sights—and it's short enough to leave time for the beach at tour's end. Kids are welcome, but little ones should sit on a grown-up's lap while on the bus.

⚓ Adults: $35 (ages 10 and above)
　Children: $24 (ages 3–9)
　Under age 3: free
　Departure Times: 8 A.M.;
　12:20 P.M.

Coral World and Island Drive
(3.5 hours; All ages)

One of the world's few underwater observatories, Coral World affords visitors the opportunity to pet a shark and touch a starfish—all without getting wet. The drive to Mountain Top is equally memorable. It's definitely one of St. Thomas's star attractions.

 It depends on whom you ask. All of us loved the aquarium. Some kids were under-enthused by the Mountain Top experience, but the grown-ups ate it up (there were shops and snack stops, plus a pretty porch overlooking Magens Bay). Some thoughts from all: Don't let small children sit on the outside of the tour vehicle—it's too easy to fall out. The more senior members of our group found Mountain Top's steep incline tough to maneuver.

⚓ Adults: $41 (ages 10 and above)
   Children: $30 (ages 3–9)
   Under age 3: free
   Departure Times: 8 A.M.;
   12 P.M.

Water Island Mountain Bike Adventure
(3.5 hours; Ages 10 and up)

Take a short boat ride to Water Island (off St. Thomas) and enjoy the beauty of the area from the seat of a mountain bike. There's a stop at the beach for swimming and relaxing after your two-wheel adventure.

 No raves. Those we talked to felt it wasn't worth the price.

⚓ Adults: $69 (ages 10 and above; not recommended for younger children)
   Departure Time: 8:45 A.M.

Sea Trek Helmet Dive at Coral World Marine Park
(3.5 hours; Ages 10 and up)

How does a leisurely, underwater stroll sound to you? Impossible? Not here. All it takes is a Sea Trek helmet, gloves, and special water shoes (and $82)— and presto! You're ready to meander among marine life at Coral World Marine Park—the Number One tourist destination in St. Thomas. The underwater part lasts about 45 minutes and is followed by 90 minutes of free time to explore the park.

Definitely a unique underwater exploration. There is an abundance of sea life to marvel at.

⚓ Adults: $82 (ages 10 and above)
Departure Time: varies

Golf at Mahogany Run
(6 hours; Ages 10 and up)

Tiger Woods wannabes will delight in this outing. The scenic, 18-hole, par-70 St. Thomas course was designed by George and Tom Fazio. It may be tough to concentrate on your game, as the amazing views almost cry out for a camera. Greens fees, a golf cart, and transportation are included; rental clubs are available for an extra charge.

Both casual and passionate golfers agree that this course is on a par with the best.

⚓ Adults: $189 (ages 10 and above; not recommended for younger children)
Departure Time: 8:15 A.M.

Screamin' Eagle Jet Boat
(1 hour; Ages 5 and up)

A 700-horse-power turbo-charged jet boat whisks guests through a scenic tour of the St. Thomas harbor and along the coastline at breathtaking speed. Hold on tight—the 45-minute ride is anything but smooth. Guests must be at least 48 inches tall to experience the *Screamin' Eagle* jet boat.

Very exhilarating! A real scream! Not for the faint of heart—or those wishing to stay dry.

⚓ Adults: $44 (ages 10 and above)
Children: $39 (ages 5–9)
Departure Times: 8:50 A.M.;
9:10 A.M.; 12:10 P.M.

Buck Island Catamaran Sail & Snorkel
(3.5 hours; Ages 5 and up)

Guests spill onto the foredeck, sunbathe, sip a complimentary beverage, and enjoy a 40-minute sail to Shipwreck Cove. Once there, the captain drops anchor and it's fin-and-goggle-donning time. The 90-minute snorkel session takes place over a sunken shipwreck.

We are always up for a sailing/snorkeling combo. And in this case, the shipwreck is an excellent bonus.

⚓ Adults: $50 (ages 10 and above)
Children: $35 (ages 5–9)
Departure Time: 8:15 A.M.

Kayak, Hike, and Snorkel of Cas Cay
(4–4.5 hours; Ages 8 and up)

Travel by van to the Virgin Islands Eco Tours Marine Sanctuary and explore its lush, tropical ecosystem aboard a two-person kayak. Guests also visit a hermit crab "village" and explore a marine tidal pool and a geologic blowhole along a coral beach. The capper is a beginner-rated, guided snorkel adventure.

 If you're fit as a fiddle, this active experience can be quite rewarding. The sanctuary is beautiful.

⚓ Adults: $69 (ages 10 and above)
   Children: $69 (ages 8–9)
   Departure Time: 8:30 A.M.

Coral World Marine Park by Land and Sea
(3.5 hours; All ages)

Okay, so the semi-sub may be a mere 8 feet under water, but the views are truly depth-defying. The adventure lasts about 45 minutes. Then you're free to spend 90 minutes exploring the marine conservation park on your own. Highlights? The Deep Reef Tank, Stingray Pool, and a three-story *underwater* observation tower.

 The park isn't St. Thomas's most famous tourist attraction for nothing. If you're not claustrophobic, there are big thrills to be had.

⚓ Adults: $44 (ages 10 and above)
   Children: $34 (ages 9 and under)
   Departure Time: varies

LAND AND SEA VACATIONS
Pairing a Walt Disney World Vacation with a Disney Cruise

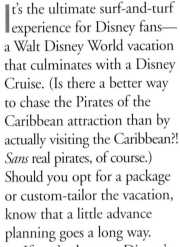

It's the ultimate surf-and-turf experience for Disney fans—a Walt Disney World vacation that culminates with a Disney Cruise. (Is there a better way to chase the Pirates of the Caribbean attraction than by actually visiting the Caribbean?! *Sans* real pirates, of course.) Should you opt for a package or custom-tailor the vacation, know that a little advance planning goes a long way.

If you've been to Disney's world before, you know that it is not a small one. In fact, it covers 40 square miles. That's nearly twice the size of Manhattan—and with about as many attractions, restaurants, and places to stay as one might expect from an area that size. We're talking four theme parks, two water parks, two dozen hotels, a dining, shopping, and entertainment district, and championship golf courses, plus boating, fishing, tennis, and more. Add a cruise to the mix and even seasoned Disney veterans run the risk of becoming overwhelmed. The good news is that Disney Cruise Line packages include just about everything you'll ever need. That frees you up to focus on a very important goal: having fun. Of course, the more ambitious vacation planners may relish the challenge of designing their own vacation. This approach, while a tad more labor-intensive, can be quite satisfying. No matter which strategy you choose, the following pages should help ensure a successful land-sea adventure.

Land-Sea Vacation Packages

7-Night Land and Sea Packages

One of the most popular ways to experience a Disney vacation, this package pairs either a 3- or 4-night stay at a Walt Disney World resort with a 3- or 4-night cruise aboard the *Disney Wonder*. (For cruise itineraries, see page 8.) It's called "Land and Sea" for a reason—the land portion of the vacation always comes first. You'll have a choice of a variety of Walt Disney World resort hotels. Expect your digs to be comparable with the category of stateroom you select on the ship. That's to say each hotel is in a certain category, based on overall value. Disney Cruise Line has paired them up with comparable stateroom categories to ensure a seamless transition. (For more information on stateroom categories, refer to page 56.)

A big plus to this package is the one-time check-in (for U.S. citizens). That means once you've checked into your resort, you'll have completed the check-in process for the *Disney Wonder*, too—and you'll get to breeze by the check-in desk at the port terminal. In fact, the powers that be are so intent on making the transition from a Disney resort to the ship seamless, that the key to your hotel room does double duty as your stateroom key (with the exception of the Swan and Dolphin resorts). This special card is known by insiders as the "Key to the World." Once onboard, you'll use it as ID, and as a charge card, too. Keep it with you at all times.

If you have Cruise-related questions while at Walt Disney World, know there is a dedicated information desk near the lobby of each of the selected WDW resorts.

Matching Disney Resort and Stateroom Categories

Resort Category	Stateroom Category
Deluxe Flagship Resort Hotel (*Grand Floridian Resort & Spa*)	1, 2, 3
Deluxe Resort Hotels (*Animal Kingdom Lodge, Beach Club, Polynesian, Saratoga Springs Resort & Spa*)	4, 5, 6, 7
Moderate Resort Hotels (*Port Orleans French Quarter* and *Riverside, Caribbean Beach*)	8, 9, 10, 11, 12

HOT TIP

Disney Cruise Vacations offer a day-before option at a non-Disney resort with some packages. For information, contact a travel agent or call 800-910-3650.

WHAT'S INCLUDED? WHAT'S NOT?

Included in the package price are the following: Walt Disney World resort accommodations, unlimited admission to all Walt Disney World theme parks, and use of the WDW transportation system for the length of your stay, plus shipboard accommodations, meals, snacks, and entertainment. (For parties reserving a Category 1 or 2 suite for more than five guests, an additional Walt Disney World hotel room will be required. There is a nightly charge for this extra room.)

What's not included? Meals and beverages at Walt Disney World, transfers to Port Canaveral (although these can be purchased in advance), airfare, shore excursions, meals ashore in ports of call (with the exception of Castaway Cay), gratuities, laundry or valet services, parking, or any other items not specifically included.

"Selected" Walt Disney World Hotels

A special group of Walt Disney World properties hold the distinction of being chosen by Disney Cruise Line as part of their land-sea vacation experience. We've stayed at all of them and can vouch for each one. Given that, if one of your favorites is not on the list, you may want to consider customizing your own cruise package (see page 214). But if the all-inclusive, ready-made package is for you, you'll need to choose one of the following resorts:

Animal Kingdom Lodge

The zebras, ostriches, and Thomson's gazelles out back are not escapees from the nearby Animal Kingdom theme park. They and their hoofed and feathered comrades live on the resort's carefully plotted pasturelands, giving round-the-clock credence to its claim as Florida's only African wildlife reserve lodge.

Romance and adventure cling to every richly appointed inch of the semicircular lodge, which serves as a five-story animal observation platform and boasts animal-viewing parlors, stellar restaurants, and an expansive swimming pool.

LOCATION: Animal Kingdom area
BIG DRAWS: Luxury laced with an undeniable spirit of adventure and romance. Amazing animal encounters.

206

Beach Club

This setting conjures up such a heady vision of turn-of-the-century Nantucket and Martha's Vineyard you'd swear you smelled salt in the air. Surely, architect Robert A.M. Stern's evocation of the grand old seaside hotels has the gulls fooled. The resort stretches along a picturesque shoreline complete with a swimming lagoon, lighthouse, and marina.

LOCATION: Epcot area
BIG DRAWS: The exceptional swimming area is second to none. Some of the World's best restaurants. Easy access to Epcot and Disney's Hollywood Studios.

DISNEY CRUISE VACATIONS AIR PROGRAM

If you plan to fly to Florida, consider allowing the Disney Cruise Vacations Air Program help you make the arrangements. In addition to lining up round-trip airfare for your whole party, they will secure motor coach ground transportation and baggage transfers. The service is available in more than 150 cities throughout the United States and Canada. For more information, call 800-910-3648. Note that the service is not included in the price of any of the vacation packages.

Caribbean Beach Resort

Note: At press time, the "deluxe" Swan and Dolphin resorts were participating in the "Land and Sea" program. That may change in 2009. For information, call 407-939-3643.

In this colorful evocation of the Caribbean, the spirit of the islands is captured by a lake ringed by beaches and villages representing Barbados, Martinique, Trinidad, Jamaica, and Aruba. Each village is marked by clusters of two-story buildings that transport you to the Caribbean, with cool pastel facades, white railings, and metallic roofs. Old Port Royale houses eateries and shops.

LOCATION: Epcot area
BIG DRAWS: Excellent value. Cheery environs with a decidedly Caribbean feel. Kids love the pirate-themed pool.

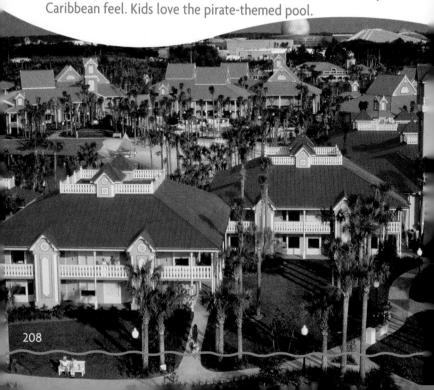

Grand Floridian Resort & Spa

A romantic slice of Victorian confectionery, this resort recalls the opulent hotels that beckoned high society at the turn of the 20th century. The Grand Floridian's central building and five guest buildings—white structures laced with verandas and turrets and topped with gabled roofs of red shingle—sprawl over acres of lakeside shorefront. Every glance embraces towering palms, stunning lake views, and rose gardens.

The impressive lobby features immense chandeliers, stained-glass skylights, and live piano and orchestra music. The resort also offers some of the best restaurants on Disney property.

LOCATION: Magic Kingdom area
BIG DRAWS: The height of luxury with a view of Cinderella Castle. And it's just one monorail stop away from the Magic Kingdom.

Polynesian

This resort echoes the romance and beauty of the South Pacific with enchanting realism. Polynesian music is piped throughout the lushly landscaped grounds, which boast white-sand beaches, torches that burn nightly, and sufficient flowers to perfume the air.

Guest buildings, which are set amid tropical gardens, are named for Pacific islands. But the resort's centerpiece is unquestionably the Great Ceremonial house, which contains a three-story garden that all but consumes the atrium lobby.

LOCATION: Magic Kingdom area
BIG DRAWS: A breathtaking, you-are-there South Seas ambience makes the "Poly" exceptionally romantic. It's connected to the Magic Kingdom via monorail and water taxi. And the volcano pool is a huge kid-pleaser.

Port Orleans Riverside

Southern hospitality takes two forms at this resort: pillared mansions with groomed lawns and upriver, rustic homes with tin roofs and bayou charm. The Sassagoula River curls around the resort's main recreation area like a moat. Bridges link guest lodgings with this area and the steamship-style building that houses the resort's eateries.

HOT TIP

Guests who book the 7-night Land and Sea Vacation have the option of adding the Disney Dining Plan when they book their trip. It allows each guest one table-service and one counter-service meal, plus one snack for each night of their WDW stay.

LOCATION: Downtown Disney area (near Epcot)
BIG DRAWS: Exceptional value. A lovely setting.

Port Orleans French Quarter

New Orleans's historic French Quarter is evoked in this resort's prim row house–style buildings, which are wrapped in ornate wrought-iron railings and set amid romantic gardens and tree-lined blocks. Guestrooms are located in seven three-story buildings. The whole enclave is set alongside a stand-in Mississippi River known as the Sassagoula.

LOCATION: Downtown Disney area (near Epcot)

BIG DRAWS: A good bang for the buck. Charming environs. It's the least sprawling of the moderate resorts. And kids get a big kick out of the pool area and serpent slide.

Saratoga Springs Resort & Spa

Long for the relaxation of a lakeside retreat—complete with fragrant gardens, bubbling fountains, and a spectacular spa? Look no further. This resort has all of the above, plus colorful Victorian architecture, rolling hills, and even a classic boardwalk. The property aims to recapture the charm and rejuvenating ambience of Saratoga Springs, New York, circa the late 1800s.

LOCATION: Downtown Disney area

BIG DRAWS: A soothing spa and lovely pool area (zero-depth entry). A 10-minute stroll to the Downtown Disney entertainment district, this resort is a Disney Vacation Club property (but available to everyone).

Customized Land and Sea Vacations

While a prepackaged vacation holds great appeal for many a traveler, some folks prefer a less restrictive approach. It's possible your favorite Walt Disney World resort isn't among the "selected" resorts included in Disney Cruise Line packages (there are, after all, two dozen different hotels to choose from). Or, perhaps, you'd rather stay somewhere outside Disney's borders. Maybe you'd like a sea-*land* vacation, as in a cruise *followed* by a stay in central Florida. Time and money no object? Consider pairing a week at Disney World with a 7-day cruise! The possibilities are virtually without limit.

For more information about Walt Disney World, including theme parks, resorts, restaurants, and more, visit *www.disneyworld.com*, call 407-W-DISNEY, or check out a copy of *Birnbaum's Official Guide to Walt Disney World 2009*.

GROUND TRANSFERS

Disney Cruise Line provides reliable friendly service aboard its motor coaches (aka: buses). Getting to the buses is easy. Upon arrival at Orlando International Airport, take a tram to the Main Terminal. Once there, proceed directly to the Disney Welcome Center. It's on Level One, Side B.

The real bonus here is the baggage handling: Disney reps will pull your tagged luggage from baggage claim and make sure it gets delivered to your room. This applies to the land-sea vacation package travelers, too—provided that they've purchased their package through Disney Cruise Line. From the airport, a bus will take you to Port Canaveral or one of the "selected" WDW hotels (see page 206). These hotels are also the pick-up points for buses headed to Port Canaveral. So, if you are staying at another Disney resort, or even off-property, you'll have to get yourself to one of the select hotels to catch the bus to the boat. Here's a rundown of pricing for ground transfers:

TRANSFER TRIP	PRICE*
Airport to select WDW resort (one-way)	Free*
Select WDW resort to Port Canaveral	$35
Round-trip from Orlando International Airport (MCO) to Port Canaveral	$69
Land and Sea Package (Orlando airport to select WDW resort; WDW resort to Port Canaveral; Port Canaveral to airport)	$69

Prices are per person, were correct at press time, and are subject to change.
* Transportation from Orlando International Airport to WDW resorts will remain free throughout 2009 (and beyond). It is provided by "Disney's Magical Express."

Walt Disney World

Whether you plan to spend three days or three weeks, chances are you'll have a tough time taking in all of Walt Disney World. The vast resort boasts four theme parks (Magic Kingdom, Epcot, Disney's Hollywood Studios, and Disney's Animal Kingdom), two water parks (Typhoon Lagoon and Blizzard Beach), golf, boating, fishing, tennis, waterskiing, parasailing, horseback riding, stock-car driving, and more.

If your time is limited to a few days, we recommend visiting the theme parks and taking in the best attractions they have to offer (see pages 219–220). If you have the luxury of time, we suggest you stagger your visits to the parks, and intersperse peaceful respites by the pool, sporting activities, and shopping sprees. In any case, you'll also want to treat yourself to a classic Disney dining experience, even if it's simply an ice-cream bar in the shape of you-know-who's head. . . .

Theme Park Tickets

The process of selecting a ticket to Walt Disney World theme parks can leave your head spinning more than a ride in a teacup. To simplify the process, ask yourself a few questions. How many days will I spend in the parks? Do I have a favorite park? Will I be making another trip to WDW this year? If you've got one day only, you should buy a one-day "Magic Your Way base ticket." That will allow you to visit one theme park for one day. Easy, right? Now, if you're going to be spending two or more days in the theme parks, it gets a bit trickier. You can purchase a multi-day (from 2- to 10-days) base ticket and customize it. Would you like to park-hop? That is, to visit

HOT TIP

Many multi-day tickets can be purchased by phone or via the Internet; call 407-824-4321, or visit *www.disneyworld.com.* There is a $3 handling fee, but it's convenient to arrive with tickets in hand. Allow at least three weeks for delivery.

more than one theme park on one day? You should purchase the "park-hopping" option. Do you plan to visit a water park during your stay? Perhaps a trip to Disney's Wide World of Sports complex, Pleasure Island, and/or DisneyQuest (the arcade at Downtown Disney West Side)? Consider adding the "Water Park Fun & More" option to your base ticket. Finally, if you might not have a chance to use all of the theme park days allotted by the ticket, ask for the "no expiration" option. This is a kind of insurance. It allows for a

little more spontaneity during your trip, since you won't be obligated to use up your entire ticket. That said, if you don't spring for the "no expiration" option, *any unused days on the ticket will expire 14 days after it is first used.* No exceptions.

Finally, there's the subject of an Annual Pass. What's that? You don't live in Florida, so how on Earth could this be worthwhile? The truth is, a premium annual pass costs about the same as a 10-day Magic Your Way ticket with all of the available bells and whistles. And, like the latter, it also includes admission to the water parks and Pleasure Island—plus a year of theme park admission. Annual passes net the bearer many discounts, including reduced resort rates. If you plan to head back to WDW within 365 days of activating your pass, it's like getting into the parks for free!

WDW RESTAURANT ROUNDUP

Walt's world is full of family-friendly dining establishments. Taking into consideration theming, value, and overall quality, these are ten of our top table-service choices:

- Biergarten (Epcot)
- Boma—Flavors of Africa (Animal Kingdom Lodge)
- Cape May Cafe* (Beach Club resort)
- Chef Mickey's* (Contemporary resort)
- Cinderella's Royal Table* (Magic Kingdom)
- Crystal Palace* (Magic Kingdom)
- 50's Prime Time Cafe (Disney's Hollywood Studios)
- Garden Grill* (Epcot)
- Rainforest Cafe (Animal Kingdom and Downtown Disney)
- Sci-Fi Dine-In Theater (Disney's Hollywood Studios)

*Disney characters are in attendance for at least one of the meals offered by the eatery.

HOT TIP

To book a table at a WDW restaurant, call 407-WDW-DINE (939-3463). Call to confirm it before you leave home!

A Whirlwind World Tour

No matter how long you plan to stay at Walt Disney World, deciding what to do first can be a challenge. When it comes to the theme parks, if we had four days, we'd visit them in this order: Magic Kingdom, Epcot, Disney's Hollywood Studios, and Animal Kingdom. Since the Magic Kingdom is our favorite (and tops with most kids), we'd be sure to hop back to it once or twice. When it comes to narrowing the list of theme park "must-sees" to the barely manageable, we recommend the following attractions and shows that we believe stand head, shoulders, and ears above the rest.

MAGIC KINGDOM*

- Splash Mountain
- Big Thunder Mountain Railroad
- Pirates of the Caribbean
- The Haunted Mansion
- Peter Pan's Flight
- Mickey's PhilharMagic
- Buzz Lightyear's Space Ranger Spin
- It's a Small World
- The Many Adventures of Winnie the Pooh
- Wishes (fireworks show)

*With young children: Dumbo the Flying Elephant, The Many Adventures of Winnie the Pooh, Mickey's PhilharMagic, It's a Small World, Cinderella's Golden Carrousel, Tomorrowland Speedway, Walt Disney World Railroad, and all of Mickey's Toontown Fair.

EPCOT*

- Soarin' (Living with the Land pavilion)
- Spaceship Earth
- Test Track
- Turtle Talk with Crush (The Seas pavilion)
- Mission: SPACE (the less intense, non-spinning version)
- IllumiNations: Reflections of Earth (fireworks show)
- The American Adventure
- Honey, I Shrunk the Audience (Imagination! pavilion)

*With young children: The Seas with Nemo & Friends and Imagination! pavilions (skip Honey, I Shrunk the Audience), Mexico's boat ride, and Kidcot Funstops.

DISNEY'S HOLLYWOOD STUDIOS*

- The Twilight Zone™ Tower of Terror
- Rock 'n' Roller Coaster
- Beauty and the Beast— Live on Stage
- Muppet*Vision 3D
- Star Tours
- Fantasmic! (a combination fireworks/stage show)
- Lights, Motors, Action! Extreme Stunt Show
- Toy Story Mania!

*With young children: Voyage of the Little Mermaid, Muppet*Vision 3D, Honey, I Shrunk the Kids Movie Set Adventure, Playhouse Disney, and Beauty and the Beast— Live on Stage.

HOT TIP

As the definitive source of insider information, we highly (and immodestly) recommend the *Birnbaum's Official Guide to Walt Disney World 2009.*

ANIMAL KINGDOM*

- Expedition Everest
- Dinosaur
- Kali River Rapids
- Kilimanjaro Safaris
- It's Tough to be a Bug!
- Festival of the Lion King
- Pangani Forest Exploration Trail
- Maharajah Jungle Trek
- Finding Nemo—the Musical
- Flights of Wonder

*With young children: The Oasis, Pocahontas & Her Forest Friends, Festival of the Lion King, DinoLand, The Boneyard playground, Maharajah Jungle Trek, Pangani Forest Exploration Trail, and the Kilimanjaro Safaris.

INDEX

A

accommodations. *see* staterooms
airplane, traveling by, 25
　Disney Cruise Vacation Air Program, 207
Aloft, *Wonder*, 73
amenities aboard Disney ships, 40
Animal Kingdom, 218, 220
Animal Kingdom Lodge (WDW), 206
Animator's Palate (restaurant), 53, 64–65

B

babies, traveling with, 29–31
　cribs, 29
　food and formulas for, 29–30
　stroller rentals, 40
babysitting services, 30
Bahamas, *see* Nassau (the Bahamas)
bars and lounges, 76–77, 80
beach activities
　Castaway Cay, 149–161
　Cozumel, 103–121
　Grand Cayman, 123–139
　Nassau, 163–173
　St. Maarten, 175–187
　St. Thomas/St. John, 189–201
Beach Club resort (WDW), 207
biking
　Castaway Cay, 156–157
　St. Maarten, 185
　St. Thomas/St. John, 196
bingo, 90–91
Birnbaum's Official Guide to Walt Disney World 2009, 214, 220
boarding, 48–49
booking a cruise aboard the *Magic* and the *Wonder*, 19–20
breakfast with Disney characters, 75, 83–84
brunch at Palo, 69
bus (Disney motor coach from WDW to Port Canaveral), 26, 28, 215
business services onboard, 38

C

camera needs, 39, 167
cancellation policy, 20
　deposit requirements, 20

Captain's Gala Dinner, 75
car, traveling by, 26–28
　driving to Port Canaveral from North Florida, 27–28
　driving to Port Canaveral from South Florida, 28
Caribbean Beach Resort (WDW), 208
cash, 39-40
　See also money matters
Castaway Cay, 149–161
　Cabana Massages, 98
　shopping on, 95
catamaran sailing
　Castaway Cay, 152
　Cozumel, 110
　Key West, 144, 147
　Nassau, 166
　St. Maarten, 177
　St. Thomas/St. John, 200
cell phones, 38
character breakfast, 75, 83–84
checking in, 44–46
children. *see* kids
Christmas sailings, 115
clothing (appropriate attire), 21
cold and flu advisory, 28
conference facilities onboard, 40
Country Inns & Suites by Carlson, 21
Cove Cafe, 73
Cozumel, Mexico, 103–121
credit cards, 19, 39–40
cribs, 29
cruise packages (itineraries), 8–13

D

deck parties, 83
dietary needs, 71
dining, 62–76
　Captain's Gala Dinner, 75
　children's menu, 72
　proper attire for dinner, 70
　reservations, 49, 67–68
　room service, 74
　"rotational dining," 64
　seating times and situations, 69–70
　self-service, fast food, and snacks, 71–74
　special dietary needs, 71
　special dining experiences, 75–76
　table service, 64–71
　wine with meals, 70–71, 76
disabilities, travelers with, 31–32

Disney characters, breakfast with, 75, 83–84
Disney Cruise Line
    gifts, 92
    phone number for reservations, 28
    rates, 15
Disney Cruise Vacation Air Program, 207
Disney Cruise Vacation Plan, travel insurance provided by, 24
Disney motor coach, 26
    ground transfers, 215
Disney's Hollywood Studios, 220
Disney's land and sea vacations, 12–13, 203–220
Diversions (sports pub), 96
Dolphin resort (WDW), 204, 208
drinking laws, 39
dry cleaning and valet services, 40, 60
duty-free shopping, 93

E

ecotourism, 139
entertainment (onboard), 49–56, 80–92
    deck parties, 83
    family entertainment, 83–84
    fun and games, 90–92
    grown-ups only, 81, 84
    just for kids, 84, 89
    stage shows, 80–82
    teens only, 89–90
Epcot, 219

F

Family Reunion Option, 37
film and camera needs, 39
film festivals at sea, 59
fireworks display (at sea), 76
float/tube rentals (Castaway Cay), 154
Flounder's Reef Nursery, 87, 89
food and formulas for babies, 29–30

G

golf, 104, 197
Goofy's Family Pool, 97
Goofy's Galley, 74
Grand Cayman, 123–138
Grand Floridian Resort & Spa (WDW), 209
Grouper Game Pavilion (Castaway Cay), 159
Guest Services (onboard), 55

H

hairdressing, 99
health club, 95–96
hiking (walking tours)
    Key West, 147
    St. Maarten, 184
    St. Thomas/St. John, 191, 198
honeymoons, 36–37
horseback riding, Cozumel, 106

I

identification (ID) papers, 23
    See also "Key to the World" card
insurance, travel, 24
Internet Cafe, 38, 40

J

jogging, 96

K

kayaking, 116, 141, 142, 150, 201
"Key to the World" card, 23, 46, 204
Key West, Florida, 141–147
kids
    entertainment for (3–12 years), 84–89
    Flounder's Reef Nursery, 87, 89
    Oceaneer Club, 53, 87–88
    Oceaneer Lab, 53, 88
    Ocean Quest, 56
kosher meals, 71

L

land and sea vacations. see Disney land and sea vacations
laundry facilities, 60
lounges. see bars and lounges
luggage, packing a day bag, 22
luggage tags, color-coded, 19, 27, 55
Lumière's, 65

M

Magic Kingdom, 219
mail, 39
manicures and pedicures, 99
marriage
    renewing your vows, 133
    See also weddings
medical matters, 28, 34–35
    cold and flu advisory, 28
    medical storage in staterooms

("cooling boxes"), 31
prescription medication, 22
money matters, 39–40
deposit requirements, 20
payment methods, 19–20
motor coach (from WDW to Port Canaveral), 26, 28–29, 215
movies (onboard), 59, 91–92

N

Nassau (the Bahamas), 163–173

O

Ocean Quest, 56
Oceaneer Club (for kids 3–7 years), 53, 87–88
registering kids for, 49
Oceaneer Lab (for kids 8–12 years), 88
registering kids for, 49
onboard shops, 54, 93–95
Orlando International Airport, 26–27

P

package deals
Photography Package, 159
packing suggestions, 21–22
Palo (adults-only restaurant), 68–69
reservations for, 49, 67–69
parasailing (Castaway Cay), 155
park hopper tickets for Walt Disney World, 216–217
Parrot Cay (restaurant), 55, 67–68
passport, 23
payment methods for Disney Cruise Vacations, 19–20
personal checks, 19
Personal Navigator, 21, 53, 55, 60, 62, 71, 78–79
pets, no-pet policy, 37
photo center, 40
Shutters (photo shop), 53
Photography Package, 159
Pinocchio's Pizzeria, 73
"Pirates IN the Caribbean" party, 75
planning your trip, 7–41
booking shore excursions, 23
booking the cruise, 19–20
cancellation policy, 20
clothing, suitable, 21
cold and flu advisory, 28
cost of your cruise, 14–16, 205

"extras" not included, 16
customized travel tips, 29–35
debarkation process, 19
deposit requirements, 20
ID requirements, 23
medical matters, 28, 34–35
packing, 21–22
payment methods, 19–20
selecting a cruise package, 7–15
selecting a stateroom, 17–18
shipboard amenities, 40
special occasions, 36–37
transportation to the ship, 25–29
travel insurance, 24
traveling with babies, 29–32
traveling with disabilities, 31–32
traveling without children, 33–34
Pluto's Dog House (snack bar), 73
Polynesian resort (WDW), 210
Port Canaveral
check-in at Terminal 8, 44–46
transportation from Orlando International Airport to, 25–28
Port Orleans French Quarter (WDW), 212
Port Orleans Riverside (WDW), 211
ports of call, 101–201
Castaway Cay, 149–161
Cozumel, Mexico, 103–121
Grand Cayman, 123–139
Key West, 141–147
Nassau (the Bahamas), 163–173
St. Maarten, 175–187
St. Thomas/St. John, 189–201
Preludes (onboard shop), 94
prescription medication, 22
Princess autograph session, 53

Q

Quarter Master's Arcade, 90
Quiet Cove (pool for adults), 96–97

R

reservations, 49
for dining onboard, 49
for shore excursions, 23
for Vista Spa & Salon, 49, 98
for WDW restaurants, 218
restaurants in Walt Disney World, 218
reunions, 37
room service, 74

S

safes (in the staterooms), 56
safety drill (on day one), 49, 61
Sail Away Celebration, 49
salon and spa, 49, 95, 97–99
St. Maarten (St. Martin), 175–187
St. Thomas/St. John, 189–201
scuba diving, 105, 170, 182, 198
secretarial services, 40
shopping
    aboard ship, 54, 93–95
    Castaway Cay, 95
    Disney Cruise Line gifts, 92
    duty-free shopping, 93
    St. Maarten/St. Martin, 175
    St. Thomas, 189
Shore Excursions desk, 55
Shutters (photo shop), 53
smoking policy, 40
snorkeling
    Castaway Cay, 152–153
    Cozumel, 106, 110, 112, 116
    Grand Cayman, 122–24, 128, 133–135, 138
    Key West, 142, 144
    Nassau, 166, 167
    St. Maarten, 176–177, 187
    St. Thomas/St. John, 190, 193–195, 199–201
spa and salon, 49, 97–99
sports and recreation aboard ship, 95–97
sports pub (Diversions), 96
Stack, the, 73
stage shows, 80–82
stamps, 39, 95
staterooms, 56–59
    matching WDW resort categories with comparable staterooms, 205
    wheelchair-accessible, 31
stroller rentals, 40
Studio Sea (family entertainment), 53, 83
Swan resort (Walt Disney World), 204, 208
swimming (onboard), 52, 96–97

T

tea
    Family Tea, 76, 84
    high tea at Palo, 69
teens-only entertainment, 73, 89–90, 158
telephone service, 41
    calling guests aboard ships, 38
    important phone numbers, 28
television channels, onboard, 59
tendering, 62
tipping (general guidelines), 41, 66
travel insurance, 24
Triton's (restaurant on the *Wonder*), 55, 66–67

U

undersea adventures
    Castaway Cay, 152–153
    Cozumel, 105, 114, 117
    Grand Cayman, 124–128, 126–127
    Key West, 142, 144
    Nassau, 166–167, 170
    St. Maarten, 176–177, 180, 182–183, 187
    St. Thomas/St. John, 190, 193–195, 197, 199–201
    See also snorkeling

V

valet service, 40
Vista Spa & Salon, 49, 97–99

W

Walt Disney Theatre, 53, 80–81
Walt Disney World (WDW)
    phone number for WDW Central Reservations, 28
    restaurant roundup, 218
    "selected" hotels at, 206–213
    theme park tickets, 216–217
weddings, 36
wheelchair-accessible staterooms, 32
wheelchairs, 31–32
Wide World of Sports Deck (deck 10), 51, 96
"Wi-Fi" service, 68
wine, Disney's wine packages, 70–71, 76
www.disneycruise.com, 20